ANDRÉ CHÉNIER
POETRY AND REVOLUTION 1792-1794

LEGENDA

LEGENDA is the Modern Humanities Research Association's book imprint for new research in the Humanities. Founded in 1995 by Malcolm Bowie and others within the University of Oxford, Legenda has always been a collaborative publishing enterprise, directly governed by scholars. The Modern Humanities Research Association (MHRA) joined this collaboration in 1998, became half-owner in 2004, in partnership with Maney Publishing and then Routledge, and has since 2016 been sole owner. Titles range from medieval texts to contemporary cinema and form a widely comparative view of the modern humanities, including works on Arabic, Catalan, English, French, German, Greek, Italian, Portuguese, Russian, Spanish, and Yiddish literature. Editorial boards and committees of more than 60 leading academic specialists work in collaboration with bodies such as the Society for French Studies, the British Comparative Literature Association and the Association of Hispanists of Great Britain & Ireland.

The MHRA encourages and promotes advanced study and research in the field of the modern humanities, especially modern European languages and literature, including English, and also cinema. It aims to break down the barriers between scholars working in different disciplines and to maintain the unity of humanistic scholarship. The Association fulfils this purpose through the publication of journals, bibliographies, monographs, critical editions, and the MHRA Style Guide, and by making grants in support of research. Membership is open to all who work in the Humanities, whether independent or in a University post, and the participation of younger colleagues entering the field is especially welcomed.

Transcript publishes books about all kinds of imagining across languages, media and cultures: translations and versions, inter-cultural and multi-lingual writing, illustrations and musical settings, adaptation for theatre, film, TV and new media, creative and critical responses. We are open to studies of any combination of languages and media, in any historical moments, and are keen to reach beyond Legenda's traditional focus on modern European languages to embrace anglophone and world cultures and the classics. We are interested in innovative critical approaches: we welcome not only the most rigorous scholarship and sharpest theory, but also modes of writing that stretch or cross the boundaries of those discourses.

TRANSCRIPT

1. *Adapting the Canon: Mediation, Visualization, Interpretation*, edited by Ann Lewis and Silke Arnold-de Simine
2. *Adapted Voices: Transpositions of Céline's Voyage au bout de la nuit and Queneau's Zazie dans le métro*, by Armelle Blin-Rolland
3. *Zola and the Art of Television: Adaptation, Recreation, Translation*, by Kate Griffiths
4. *Comparative Encounters between Artaud, Michaux and the Zhuangzi: Rationality, Cosmology and Ethics*, by Xiaofan Amy Li
5. *Minding Borders: Resilient Divisions in Literature, the Body and the Academy*, edited by Nicola Gardini, Adriana Jacobs, Ben Morgan, Mohamed-Salah Omri and Matthew Reynolds
6. *Memory Across Borders: Nabokov, Perec, Chamoiseau*, by Sara-Louise Cooper
7. *Erotic Literature in Adaptation and Translation*, edited by Johannes D. Kaminski
8. *Translating Petrarch's Poetry: L'Aura del Petrarca from the Quattrocento to the 21st Century*, edited by Carole Birkan-Berz, Guillaume Coatalen and Thomas Vuong
9. *Making Masud Khan: Psychoanalysis, Empire and Modernist Culture*, by Benjamin Poore
10. *Prismatic Translation*, edited by Matthew Reynolds
11. *The Patient, the Impostor and the Seducer: Medieval European Literature in Hebrew*, by Tovi Bibring
12. *Reading Dante and Proust by Analogy*, by Julia Caterina Hartley
13. *The First English Translations of Molière: Drama in Flux 1663-1732*, by Suzanne Jones
14. *After Clarice: Reading Lispector's Legacy in the Twenty-First Century*, edited by Adriana X. Jacobs and Claire Williams
15. *Uruguayan Theatre in Translation: Theory and Practice*, by Sophie Stevens
16. *Hamlet Translations: Prisms of Cultural Encounters across the Globe*, edited by Márta Minier and Lily Kahn
17. *The Foreign Connection: Writings on Poetry, Art and Translation*, by Jamie McKendrick
18. *Poetics, Performance and Politics in French and Italian Renaissance Comedy*, by Lucy Rayfield

André Chénier

Poetry and Revolution 1792–1794

A Bilingual Edition of the
Last Poems with New Translations

❖

DAVID McCALLAM

LEGENDA

Transcript 24
Modern Humanities Research Association
2021

Published by Legenda
an imprint of the Modern Humanities Research Association
Salisbury House, Station Road, Cambridge CB1 2LA

ISBN 978-1-83954-016-5 (HB)
ISBN 978-1-83954-017-2 (PB)

First published 2021

Copy-Editor: Charlotte Brown

CONTENTS

❖

ACKNOWLEDGEMENTS

❖

I have taught and researched the poetry of André Chénier for many years now. Successive classes of brilliant students in French at the University of Sheffield have opened my eyes to new understandings of his revolutionary poems, and I am grateful to them for it. Along the way I have also benefitted from the expertise and advice of colleagues in French and English at Sheffield. I owe a particular debt of gratitude to my former colleague Helen Abbott and the poet Eleanor Brown who contributed to a translation workshop on Chénier's last poems and inspired new insights into the verse. This book also owes a good deal to the meticulous reading and perceptive commentary that Catriona Seth kindly brought to a first draft. Bob Derksen was my Canadian poetry guru on certain poems, especially the translation of 'A Versailles'; so many thanks are owed to him. I am, as ever, grateful in ways beyond this little book for the presence and love in my life of my daughter Eve and son Isaac. Above all, my wonderful wife Renata Schellenberg remains my muse — though she won't thank me for saying that. Finally, I dedicate this work to the memory of Terry Pratt, a great teacher and lover of French poetry who, many years ago, gave me his personal copy of Chénier's *Œuvres complètes*, which I have used as my primary text. It is worn and dog-eared now, but still clearly carries Terry's signature, dated 'Paris, Jan 1970'.

D.M., January 2021

INTRODUCTION

❖

It is a grand object — the very *poetry* of politics.

Revolution

Just after midnight on 8 March 1794, the suspect André Chénier was made to sit at a table in a small house in Passy. Opposite him sat Nicolas Guénot, an agent of the internal state security police. Behind Guénot stood two of his assistants while a third, Duchesne, sat at a desk preparing to transcribe in phonetic French the interrogation. They had come to arrest the marquis de Pastoret whose mother-in-law lived in the house. The marquis had long since gone. But on the doorstep they had met a stocky, balding man leaving the building. He had given them evasive and contradictory answers. So he was taken back inside while the rest of the house was searched. When no one else was found, except the mother-in-law and her daughter, a message was sent to Paris to prepare the suspect's arrest warrant and his interrogation began:

Guénot: Name?
Chénier: André Chénier.
Guénot: Place of birth?
Chénier: Constantinople.
Guénot: ... Age?
Chénier: 31.
Guénot: Address?
Chénier: Rue de Cléry, Brutus section.
Guénot: How long have you lived there?
Chénier: Since 1792, at least.
Guénot: How do you earn your living?
Chénier: Since 1790 I've been living off an allowance from my father.
Guénot: How much does he give you?
Chénier: As much as is needed when I need it.
Guénot: Tell us how much a year.
Chénier: I don't know for certain. Between 800 and 1000 livres.
Guénot: Do you have any other money?
Chénier: No, nothing else.
Guénot: Where do you take your meals?
Chénier: Sometimes at my father's, sometimes at friends' and sometimes I eat out.
Guénot: What friends?
Chénier: There are several. You don't need to know their names.[2]

★   ★   ★   ★   ★

The Revolution was not just an unprecedented socio-political upheaval for France. It was also a profoundly *existential* crisis for those who lived it day by day. The Revolution comprised the dizzyingly modern realization that one's meaning in the world is often little more than the paper-thin credibility it carries in the eyes of others. The Terror is then a mesh of micro-acts, at once thrillingly chosen and horribly contingent. We come at the Revolution from the safety of history and blithely ignore the inscrutable open-endedness of every moment, the raw immediacy of the future facing its protagonists. For them the Revolution was unfolding in many different directions simultaneously. This situation generates the forms of deadly folly passed off as reason that Chénier enumerates in his nonsense verse 'J'ai lu qu'un batelier' — the serial absurdities of a world leached of meaning. In another of his iambics, 'Quand au mouton bêlant', the poet depicts the vertigo that such meaninglessness induces in its more lucid observers. A single hemistich suffices: 'Mais tout est précipice'. Stephen Romer translates this interestingly as 'But everywhere falls sheer'.[3] 'Sheer' is an apposite word here: both precipitous and complete or absolute. And what 'falls sheer' in 1794 is of course the guillotine blade, evoking its English homophone 'shear', although the key term in this sentence is probably 'everywhere', since it conveys the ubiquity of the guillotine's action in the contemporary imagination. And if everywhere is falling sheer, there is no purchase at all anywhere — this is pure vertigo, utter free fall.

★   ★   ★   ★   ★

The most famous portrait of André Chénier was painted by the Flemish artist, Joseph-Benoît Suvée, who was incarcerated with the poet in Saint-Lazare prison.[4] It is a portrait taken from life and dated 17 July 1794, just eight days before its subject's execution. It adorns most books and articles about Chénier. It shows a broad face angled defiantly towards the artist, framed in thinning dark hair over a loose white collar and striped necktie. The eyebrows are strikingly dark and strong. Given this colouring, I had always thought Chénier had brown eyes. Yet his prison entry record from 9 March 1794 is categorical: 'yeux gris bleu'.[5] He had grey-blue eyes. Chénier's eyes were greyish blue or bluish grey. For some reason, this moves me. The endlessly surprising otherness of the other.

★   ★   ★   ★   ★

The apparent paradox of André Chénier in the Revolution is that of the poet identifying with the mass of victims of the Terror in order to find his own unique voice.[6] As such, his lone voice is choral, amplifying those silenced by revolutionary violence. The choral nature of his poetry is thematic, 'Tant de morts et de pleurs, de cendres, de décombres, | Qui contre vous lèvent la voix' — voices in unison that reverse the dynamics of revolutionary victimhood, allowing the dead and those who mourn them to judge their judges.[7] The chorus is also a formal element in Chénier's poetry, which deploys the Pindaric ode, involving voices combining across a proscenium or public stage (see 'O mon esprit, au sein des cieux'). And yet this polyphonic voice conveys a conception of the Revolution which is extremely awkward, if not impossible, to co-opt into later political movements for or against the Revolution (for example, those of moderate liberals or nationalist reactionaries). Chénier's choral voice is resolutely neither pro-revolutionary nor counter-revolutionary. This is because it is founded on a value system presented as a shared good but which exists primarily in the poet's *moi*, in his own unique set of beliefs and actions. We could call it 'alter-revolutionary'. What is certain is that it arises from an abiding faith in *a* Revolution that compels the poet to resist *the* Revolution.

★   ★   ★   ★   ★

Neo-classical tragedies in eighteenth-century France often convey a weaker notion of fatefulness by making room for human superstition, ignorance and fanaticism as motivations for their terrible denouement. They lack the crushing inevitability of a dire prophecy coming true or the sheer unpredictability of an amoral god's whim. Even as it is lived contingently — or *because* it is lived contingently — the Revolution restores this sense of implacable fatefulness. Even as it claims to be history-in-the-making, it reconnects with myth. Camille Desmoulins, who practised a form of lethal journalism in 1793 that became a form of suicidal journalism in 1794, told his father in the summer of 1793: 'My turn will come'.[8] This tone of resigned fatality is echoed in Chénier's 'Comme un dernier rayon', traditionally held to be his last verse written before going to his death: 'Peut-être est-ce bientôt mon tour'. You could argue that the 'peut-être' here offers an illusory glimmer of hope, the inversion of 'est-ce' a chance for luck to turn; or, as it develops, that this last of the prison poems is ultimately more concerned with urging angry resistance and calling down terrible vengeance on his Jacobin oppressors than it is with stoic fatalism.

However, the poem's last line is not in fact the last line in Chénier's manuscripts smuggled out of prison. This is instead the pitiless coda 'Ce sera toi demain, insensible imbécile', a line that is usually appended to the iambics, 'On vit; on vit infâme'.[9] It is a grammatical sentence and a prophetic sentence with no right of appeal, the living body already anticipating the grave in its state of unfeeling stupor. This line of verse is made all the more devastating when attached to the final iambic couplet of 'On vit; on vit infâme':

> Chacun frissonne, écoute; et chacun avec joie
> Voit que ce n'est pas encor lui:
> Ce sera toi demain, insensible imbécile.

As a terrible rejoinder here, the death sentence, so to speak — 'Ce sera toi demain, insensible imbécile' — crushes mercilessly the temporary relief, released by the enjambement 'avec joie | Voit', of the preceding lines. The small distracted, consoling groups of prisoners described earlier in the poem have already been dissolved into terrified, isolated units ('chacun', 'chacun') with the arrival of the revolutionary official carrying his list of names for summary trial that day. What the death sentence then exposes is the giddy illogicality of each of the inmates trembling and listening and each of them overcome with perverse glee on hearing it is not yet his or her turn. Yet at least one of them will have been called out — and being called out is already dead to his or her fellow prisoners. This is yet another way in which Chénier articulates the intractable fate, the fully restored sense of tragedy, that overhung his contemporaries in the Terror.

★   ★   ★   ★   ★

Guénot: How long have you known the owners of this house?
Chénier: Four or five years.
Guénot: How did you meet them?
Chénier: At Citizeness Trudaine's house.
Guénot: Where does she live?
Chénier: Place de la Révolution. It's the side house.
Guénot: How do you know the Side house, the people who live there?
Chénier: I'm a childhood friend of theirs.
Guénot: That's not right though, is it? Because in the Place de la Révolution, there's no Side household there, as you just said there was.
Chénier: I mean the house on the side of the square, next to Citizen Letemps.
Guénot: So you're bullshitting us again, since you said twice it was the Side house.
Chénier: I'm telling you the truth.

★   ★   ★   ★   ★

However much one is swayed by Chénier's poetry, there are other ways of interpreting the Revolution, alternative truths regarding its actors and events. For instance, it is equally plausible to claim that the most heroic undertaking of the Revolution was that of the 'great' Committee of Public Safety of Year II (Summer 1793-Summer 1794). This extraordinary executive composed of eleven principal members galvanized the revolutionary Republic into ceaseless action in the face of a European coalition of monarchies ranged against them, with civil war ravaging the south and west of the country, and very real counter-revolutionary intrigues undermining its popular support.[10] Working on average fifteen to eighteen hours a day, dealing with up to 600 different matters in any twenty-four-hour period, committee members often took turns to sleep on one of two camp beds installed in their main meeting room. They expended prodigious amounts of energy in their common mission, reorganizing and renewing the army, navy, religion, festivals, education, industry, science, economy, police and the arts. Their self-abnegation for the greater cause was total. This was revolutionary virtue in action. Nor was this, as it was later portrayed, the dictatorship of one man, Robespierre, seconded by his craven acolytes. All of the committee's 2,000 and more letters and orders were co-signed by at least three members. And if the committee constituted in reality a dictatorship, this was on the Roman model, not that of twentieth-century totalitarian states: an emergency military government fully sanctioned by the Convention acting as the democratic representation of the sovereign people, a government whose mandate was operative only as long as the war lasted. If the radical constitution of 1793 was suspended, the membership of the Committee of Public Safety was nonetheless submitted to scrutiny and renewal by the Convention every month. Its members might have had different talents, diverse flaws and divergent political ambitions, but they shared a common mission and pursued it together relentlessly.[11]

So next to Chénier's bête noire, the brutal and voluble Collot d'Herbois, worked the modest and conscientious Robert Lindet while the northern laconism of Antoine Saint-Just was offset by the chatty bonhomie of the southerner Bertrand Barère. Collectively they formed an exceptional model of collegial governance. The Terror that they instituted was neither inevitable nor mercilessly ideological, as some revisionist accounts maintain. It was at least as much the result of the vagaries of circumstance and personality. And far from being a capitulation to the unbridled forces of popular violence, Terrorist rule established the legal means to channel it and avoid its worst excesses.[12] We must also remember that the Terrorists were ultimately history's vanquished, defamed retroactively in the undignified scramble of Thermidor in which revolutionaries of all stripes sought to exculpate themselves by incriminating others in a potlatch of self-serving victimhood that stands as the antithesis of the self-sacrificing heroism of the great Committee. For good or ill, Chénier's last poems feed into this same Thermidorian narrative. However, not everyone forgot what had been achieved in 1793–94. In 1813, waiting with Napoleon's lackeys for the outcome of yet another futile bloodbath that dwarfed the body count of the Terror, the former member of the Committee of Public Safety of Year II, the austere Jean Bon Saint-André reminded his audience of the Herculean work the committee had accomplished. 'This was the stamp of men that saved France. I was one of them, *messieurs*'.[13]

★   ★   ★   ★   ★

We need to read André Chénier because we need to apprehend (comprehension is not possible) what it is like to *be* in a death cell during the Terror. How unique and how universal.

★   ★   ★   ★   ★

The last Classicist. The first Romantic. A neo-Classicist? A pre-Romantic? The old French literature manuals like to elide as much as possible the years 1789–99. Yet they couldn't ignore Chénier's contribution to French poetry, so he had to belong to either a 'before' or an 'after', cleaving to the Classics or foreshadowing the Romantics. This too is an ideological choice: to overlay and efface the politics of Revolution with the tradition of literature. It is a revisionist and negationist strategy; and it fundamentally disqualifies the poet's lived and written experience. Chénier is a poet in the Revolution and a poet of the Revolution. To pretend otherwise is to deny the legitimacy of his historical moment and the authenticity of his poetic voice. It also reveals how the literary categories of Classicism and Romanticism are fabricated retrospectively and applied ideologically. The ethical and aesthetic qualities that are loosely defined as classical or Romantic coexist in late eighteenth-century France and obtain simultaneously in many of its greatest works before the Revolution and in the Revolution.

★   ★   ★   ★   ★

André Chénier's life is often overdetermined by his death. Thus it is tempting to read it like a legend, imbuing its final destination with an aura of destiny — the ineluctable meeting with the guillotine on 25 July 1794. That Chénier's death makes sense of his life is compounded by the rituals of the guillotine itself. Like Charlotte Corday and other *guillotinés*, the poet had his portrait painted in prison a few days before his death. Yet, as Daniel Arasse has argued, it is the guillotine which acts as the ultimate portraitist, or the yet more modern photographer, its falling blade a crude camera shutter allowing the severed head to be held aloft and the crowd to see the face fixed in its last moment and for posterity, the traitor finally unmasked or the martyr haloed.[14] Death thus confers a proof of authenticity on the victim, an authenticity that was insistently sought and claimed in life equally by the moderate monarchist Chénier and the radical Terrorist Saint-Just. In the poet's case, however, this reversal of perspective, starting from the end-point, is of a piece with his own proleptic imagination. We might read his life through his death in the same way that he began his great verse projects, such as 'Hermès', by drafting their epilogues.[15]

★　★　★　★　★

By intuition or instruction, Nicolas Guénot interrogated André Chénier about his meals, where he took them and with whom he ate. The intuition here is that commensality — the practice of eating together — is potentially subversive. To share someone's food connotes ingesting someone's ideas. The instruction that Guénot might have received was that private dinners were the favoured occasion for counter-revolutionary plotting. In the same month that Chénier was arrested, Antoine Saint-Just carried out two devastating public indictments of opposing extremist and moderate revolutionary factions. In these prosecutions, Saint-Just cited respectively ostentatious over-eating in a time of food shortages as proof of 'aristocratic' hypocrisy, and lavish private dinners as cover for anti-republican conspiracy.[16] Eating is obviously about sustenance but it is also a metaphor of intimate internalization. The question posed by Guénot to Chénier was near the mark of his counter-revolutionary activity, it just took aim at the wrong dinners.

In September 1792, the poet-journalist fled Paris to escape the popular violence of the prison massacres in Paris as they spread to Versailles. He went first to Rouen where we know in which district and with whom he lodged. However, he then travelled on to Le Havre under an alias and there dined in the select company of persons unknown at the house of a 'bon vieux excellent homme' to whom his father had directed him.[17] This secret meeting over dinner forms the *secretum secretorum* of Chénier's revolutionary engagements. It constitutes an unknowable space into which we might project our wildest imaginings. A plot to abduct Louis XVI and spirit him abroad? A plan to assassinate prominent republican *députés*? Escape to America? The subject matter of the secrets is less important than the practices of secrecy (the alias, private conversations, intimate dinners). Interiorization of any sort is the enemy of the transparent Republic. Chénier thus contributes to the Revolution becoming an infinite Russian doll of conspiracy plots.

★　★　★　★　★

Guénot:	Do you often eat here, in this house?
Chénier:	I don't think I've ever eaten here. But I've eaten with the owners a few times in Paris.
Guénot:	Have you had any correspondence with enemy powers? The truth.
Chénier:	None.
Guénot:	So you haven't received any letters from England since you returned to the Republic?
Chénier:	One or two from Citizen Barthélemy when he was working in the embassy in England. But no others.
Guénot:	When did you receive those letters? Show them to us.
Chénier:	I don't have them.
Guénot:	What did you do with them? Why did you get rid of them?
Chénier:	It was just personal correspondence, asking to return my books and effects. Not the sort of thing one keeps.
Guénot:	Why wouldn't you keep personal letters? The truth.
Chénier:	It seems to me that letters letting one know that one's things have arrived are not worth keeping once one's things have arrived.
Guénot:	But that's not right. Because these letters are proof for both sender and receiver, so they're still valuable.
Chénier:	For private individuals, who don't need to keep their accounts in order like a small business does, when these individuals have received what was sent to them, the paperwork's not much use after that. I think that's how most people behave.
Guénot:	We're not talking about a small business here — but the important business of why you've been arrested.
Chénier:	I've no idea why I've been arrested.
Guénot:	Why are you bullshitting us? We want straight answers.
Chénier:	I'm telling you the truth. As simply as I can.

★   ★   ★   ★   ★

André Chénier was not tried and executed as a poet but as the 'salaried hack of a tyrant', as the 'editor of the supplement to the *Journal de Paris*' published to mislead and corrupt public opinion and foment counter-Revolution.[18] The two poems published in his lifetime appear as offshoots of this same anti-Jacobin journalism of 1791–92. The odes and iambics written in 1793–94 were similarly inspired by specific reports in the revolutionary press. His poetry is thus informed by what Francis Scarfe calls 'a kind of *anti-poetry*' drawn from the ephemera and topicality of news items; literature's essence as 'news that stays news' returns to its source and flirts with the obscure references and inbuilt obsolescence of revolutionary news-sheets.[19] But it would be wrong to see the verse as deriving from the journalism. Journalism and poetry spring equally from the same compulsion to bear witness. Both are suspicious of history's integrity to relate the story of the Revolution and so both offer alternative modes of 'knowing' the lived experience of these tumultuous times. Yet if Chénier's poetry and prose often share the same fount of strong negative emotions — particularly a sustained rage at the rise of revolutionary demagoguery — his poetry benefits from a more formal detachment from the present moment of expression. Distilled by its masterful play of sound and metre, an affective resonance is set up between the poem and its reader, regardless of the latter's political conviction, which persuades more subtly and more enduringly that the most impassioned journalistic rhetoric.

★ ★ ★ ★ ★

'Toi, Vertu, pleure si je meurs'. It is easy to see the poet's hailing of 'Virtue' in July 1794 as a defiant final appropriation of this central tenet of the Jacobin creed, to be realized in his execution as the proof of its absence in his persecutors. For Robespierre as for many revolutionary politicians, virtue was a public claim for moral legitimacy independent of any social institution, owing no allegiance to anything but the greater good they professed. The revolutionary man of virtue (it was also a highly gendered quality) was thus to be judged by how far he made his 'virtual' Revolution an actual realization of this greater good, to what degree his intentions were transformed into actions, his words into deeds; by how far he *appeared* to efface himself in the interests of the common weal. What Chénier's arrogation of virtue revealed in 1794 was that the discourse of virtue was as much about self-affirmation as self-sacrifice. Its mark is never just about owing allegiance to the most idealized form of general good but also about always holding true to a certain vision of oneself. To expose the hypocrisy of his revolutionary enemies, the poet fully assumes the egotistical implications of this conception of virtue as it evolves in his last poems into an animating principle of an individualized 'greatness of soul'. As such, it has a literary as much as a political genealogy, exemplified by the heroes of Corneille's tragedies whose self-sacrifice is always an act of glorious self-validation, possibly emerging again in Stendhal's doomed and defiant Romantic protagonists.

★ ★ ★ ★ ★

Guénot:	Do you live alone in your lodgings at... 97 rue de Cléry?
Chénier:	I live with my father, my mother and my older brother.
Guénot:	Any servants?
Chénier:	Just one, who looks after all four of us.
Guénot:	Where were you on 10 August 1792?
Chénier:	I was sick with severe stomach pains and nausea, brought on by kidney stones.
Guénot:	Have you suffered from this for a long time or did you just happen to have it on 10 August 1792?
Chénier:	I was getting over a bad attack of it at the time. I've had it more or less badly since I was twenty.
Guénot:	What sort of illness is it again? And which doctor treated you? Is he still treating you for it?
Chénier:	At the start of the illness I saw Dr Joffroy. But since then I've followed a diet to manage this sort of ailment.
Guénot:	Is it an illness or an ailment that you get?
Chénier:	What I get are more or less violent attacks of pain, so that I'm too ill to do anything.
Guénot:	When did you start seeing this doctor you mentioned and when did you stop? Show us your medical certificates.

Chénier: My family can certify for me, as he's the family doctor.
Guénot: Did you stand guard on 10 August 1792?
Chénier: I stood guard when my health let me.
Guénot: And on 10 August 1792 when you heard the call to arms, did you take up arms and come to the defence of your fellow citizens and to save the homeland?
Chénier: I was still too weak.
Guénot: What exactly stopped you?
Chénier: My health was too weak at the time.
Guénot: So prove it to us by giving us the medical certificates signed by the doctor of your section, since you won't give us straight answers.
Chénier: I don't have any.
Guénot: How come you don't have any?
Chénier: I don't have those medical certificates.

★   ★   ★   ★   ★

We can only come at the truth of André Chénier and the Revolution obliquely. It is like the slant of the guillotine blade. Different shapes of hatchet were initially trialled on convicts' corpses in the hospital yard at Bicêtre before concluding that the slanted blade cut most efficiently. Hence the glinting diagonal suspended over Paris, a slash between the organic/mechanic, human/inhuman, life/death. Yet its fall happens so quickly. The crowd see a chop, when in reality it is a slice. This is the oblique truth found in Gothic fiction where the stroke of the blade — less the guillotine itself than its substitutes (knife, scalpel, razor) — is slowed and savoured in all its horror. The observation of its action is thus unflinchingly more acute. This is the truth of literature's indirection. As the poet-translator Pierre Albert-Birot put it, 'la vraie vérité est à côté de la vérité' [the true truth is beside the truth].[20]

★   ★   ★   ★   ★

There were approximately 700 inmates, including about 100 women, in Saint-Lazare prison in the early summer of 1794.[21] There were approximately 700 representatives in the Convention in 1794. Coincidence? In Chénier's poem 'On vit; on vit infâme' a direct equation is established between prison and parliament, as two engines of hot air. Yet the precise figure of 700 in the manuscript poem is encoded in Persian as *heftsad* (just as the name 'Barère' is transposed into Arabic), a double obfuscation in case of discovery or a double orientalization of revolutionary 'despotism'.[22]

★   ★   ★   ★   ★

In 'L'Invention' of 1787 Chénier writes: 'Eh bien! l'âme est partout; la pensée a des ailes' [And so! the soul is everywhere; thought has wings].[23] In 1802 his fellow pantheist William Wordsworth would note, 'The objects of a poet's thoughts are everywhere [...] wheresoever he can find an atmosphere of sensation in which to move his wings'.[24] The 'âme' or soul is a numinous energy suffusing all matter, taking wing on poetic thought and voice. It is not the immortal, immaterial essence animating an individual in life and sloughing its mortal, meaty sheath in death. All things — humans, animals, insects, trees, rocks, rivers, seas, air — bathe in a common soul. It could be called 'nature', although this term does not fully acknowledge its dynamism. Better to say it is an ecology of interrelating natural forces.

So how does this soul fare in the Revolution? Chénier locates its activity in specific individuals such as the murderess Charlotte Corday. Her 'âme impénétrable' concealed her secret resolution to assassinate Jean-Paul Marat and drove her on to carry out her crime. Her soul is likened to a storm massing in a clear sky, it is Wordsworth's 'atmosphere of sensation' building to an extreme pitch, a sublime energy that overspills into her decisive counter-revolutionary act. In Chénier's 'Voûtes du Panthéon', this is complemented by an image of Marat's own soul leaving his body as a whirling black cloud of blood, filth and trash. This is not an affirmation of the soul as immaterial deathless essence but a migration of matter into matter, revealing the fundamental baseness of Marat's being. The key term is then 'whirling' ('tournoyer') insofar as the soul is the expression — here the 'exhalaisons' or expiration — of a quantum of universal divine energy. This notion of soul is thus hosted in driven and active individuals, acting through them, but it is not proper to them and is held in common by all things in existence. As a result, the soul can also operate in the collective. For Chénier, it finds expression in the bloodlust of the revolutionary mob flocking to see the guillotine in action. Nor does this bloodlust die with them, as the notes for an unfinished iambics contend, since 'leur âme passe au corps des loups et des panthères' in a 'humanimal' metempsychosis or transfer of vicious energies from the barbarous multitude to packs of ravenous wolves and panthers.[25] The opposite of this circulation of vital powers then is a particular or general listlessness or enervation. It is the lethargic poet's 'âme flétrie' or withered soul, or the passive majority that let the Jacobins hold sway by their shameful inaction, 'eunuques vils, troupeau lâche et sans âme'. The term 'lâche' here, recurrent in the last poems, doubles up its primary sense of 'cowardly' with a secondary sense of 'slack' or 'loose', lacking tensile strength, emptied of vital force, devoid of soul.

Many revolutionaries shared Chénier's conception of the soul, especially in its collective, public manifestations. It is a common energy, embodied in (the) people, a new public-spiritedness or *civisme* to be directed by revolutionary practices to shape a modern sensibility which would be bequeathed from generation to generation. 'Soul' is the revolutionary zeitgeist.[26] It is most on show where it is most manipulated: in the regime's legislation for a new appreciation of the fundamental dimensions of lived experience — space (renamed streets, new monuments, metric weights and measures) and time (smelting of church bells, revolutionary calendar, decimal clocks).

★   ★   ★   ★   ★

Guénot: So, at a time when even the lame and infirm were taking up arms
             and gathering in public squares with all the other good citizens to
             defend the homeland against the lackeys of the former king and his
             royalists, you did not do your duty as a citizen. You didn't come to
             the defence of the homeland.
Chénier: I wasn't physically strong enough to do it.
Guénot: And did your brothers and your father join in with the other
             citizens of their section to take up defensive positions against those
             tyrannizing the Republic? The truth.
Chénier: My father was old but was active in his section, and my brother was
             vice-consul in Spain. My other brothers don't live with us, so I
             don't know where they were.
Guénot: And where was your servant on 10 August 1792?
Chénier: I don't know.
Guénot: All good citizens know where they were on that day, and all the
             good citizens who heard the call to arms answered it so that they
             could help save the Republic.
Chénier: I've told you the whole truth.
Guénot: What whole truth?
Chénier: Everything I've told you.

*The transcript of the interrogation was then read back to Chénier and signed formally
by the four police agents: Guénot (chief investigator), Cramoisin, Boudgoust, Duchesne.*

Guénot: Sign it.
Chénier: No.

★   ★   ★   ★   ★

Poetry

In his last poems, Chénier turns against the Jacobins the nominative and performative speech acts of their own revolutionary language, arrogating to his verse
the lethal efficacy of a Terrorist arrest warrant or death sentence. In lines like 'Au
pied de l'échafaud j'essaye encore ma lyre', the poet 'sings' the Terror in the same
way that Homer 'sang' the Trojan War, although Chénier's song is sung to enact
the annihilation of his political foes, 'Pour *cracher* sur leurs noms, pour *chanter*
leur supplice' (my emphasis). Spitting is perhaps the most visceral aspect of this
performance — not to un-name the Jacobins in a Roman *damnatio memoriae*, but to
de-face and de-fame them physically and figuratively.

As a vulgar act, spitting is on a par with Chénier's further subversion of
revolutionary speech acts insofar as his poetry occasionally incorporates the crude
profanities peppering the populist press in the Revolution. This clearly has a
rhetorical shock value. But in turning swear-words into poetic diction, Chénier
also hints at the degradation of the exalted oath-taking that most famously
founded the revolutionary National Assembly in June 1789, an oath-taking he
extolled in his sprawling Pindaric ode, 'Le Jeu de Paume' (1791). The glorious
collective speech-act of the so-called 'Tennis Court Oath' thus degenerates into
the perfunctory swearing-in of sans-culotte juries for the show-trials of the Terror,

including Chénier's own. Swearing an oath is debased into the casual swearing of 'oaths' littering extremist news-sheets; revolutionary sacrality lapses into everyday profanity.

However, the jarring juxtaposition of foul language with classical allusions and lofty poetic collocations is about more than just shocking the reader. The vernacular turns of phrase irrupt relatively rarely, and always strategically, into Chénier's verse and fulfil particular poetic functions in the poems in which they appear. Take the example of his poem 'Voûtes du Panthéon' and its penultimate quatrain of iambics deploying a vulgar expression worthy of the populist ventriloquy of Jacques-René Hébert's *Père Duchesne* whose revolutionary language scans with phatic 'bougre' and 'foutre':

> Mais non; nous entendrons ces oraisons funèbres
> De la bouche du bon Garat;
> Puis tu [le gibet] les enverras tous au fond des ténèbres
> *Lécher le cul* du bon Marat.

The verse turns here on the verb 'lécher', to lick, as it provides the oral link between Garat's mouth and Marat's arse. It is another way of saying that any praise of Marat is talking shit. Whatever comes out of Garat's mouth is fit to disappear up the dark fundament ('au fond des ténèbres') of his hero. This scatological irreverence is heightened by the extreme *rime riche* of 'du bon Garat | du bon Marat', which expands here into the comic extravagance of the *rime rare*. The rhyming of the revolutionaries' proper names has the double effect of, firstly, suggesting that their equivalence in language signifies their equivalence as persons, as objects of a mocking and degrading nominative determinism; and secondly, it invites a search for any referential value in each name, which necessarily finds none other than their ringing echo. This further evacuates the repetition of 'bon [...] bon' of its positive meaning so that it comes ironically to signify its exact opposite — twice. Both revolutionaries are the incarnation of a worthless, pointless noise. As their contemporary Marmontel defines irony, it is 'une espèce de contre-vérité en dérision'.[27]

A more subtle, but perhaps even more effective, co-option of common speech into Chénier's poetry occurs in his iambics 'Vingt barques, faux tissus de planches fugitives'. Confronted with the murderous cruelty of the revolutionary officials who presided over the mass drownings in Nantes in late 1793 and early 1794, the poet is appalled at their manifest inhumanity, a moral vacuum filled by basest physical appetites:

> Quel remords agite le flanc,
> Tourmente le sommeil du [tribunal] impie
> Qui mange, boit, *rote* du sang? (my emphasis)

The colourful vernacular 'rote du sang', or 'belch up blood', delivers something of the animal uncouthness of the Terrorists who oversaw mass murder, something of their insatiable, over-reaching greed for drink, food and human blood. (The cannibalistic figure evoked here is a common dehumanizing device of both counter-revolutionary and revolutionary rhetoric.) What is more, the way in which this gluttonous consumption of human suffering scans in this last line mimics the revolutionaries' belching, 'Qui mang/e, boit/, rot/e du sang', as 2/2/1/3, a sort of syncopation on 'rote' that replicates the sense of blood repeating on those who quaff it with drunken abandon. As a sort of reflux of the stresses in the line, it also replicates the gasping of the victims drowning in the freezing Loire, their last lungful of air bubbling to the surface of the river.

★   ★   ★   ★   ★

The beautiful syllogism: all metaphor is poetry; all metaphor is translation; therefore all poetry is translation (and vice versa).

★   ★   ★   ★   ★

The golden rule for Chénier in poetry as in politics is to cleave to the bonds that free. That is, in politics there can be no liberty without the rule of law, so the Revolution must be at once a common release and a collective restraining of popular passions. A radical overhaul of society, yes, but only as construed and constrained by the constitution and the new legal order. In poetry the bonds that free are many — metre, rhyme, stanza, genre, etc. The poet must master them by reading attentively those who have already done so and learn by imitation. This in turn suggests that the only way to escape slavish imitation is to engage in it creatively. Hence Chénier's credo of 'l'imitation inventrice', or creative imitation, itself borrowed from Louis Racine and Edward Young.[28] It is only by fully embracing the formal constraints of poetry that one sets one's own poetic voice free; it is only by imitation that one becomes original. The poet thus discovers that his or her 'original' model does not owe its originality to any inherent qualities it possesses, but to its own innovative amalgamation of various sources and influences. More counter-intuitively, the 'original' text is invested with the originality that the poet's fresh interpretation and creative imitation bring to it.

★   ★   ★   ★   ★

In practice, Chénier's prosody returns to prose or emerges from it. His manuscripts provide examples of a prose frame that resolves itself suddenly into verse or vice versa. For instance, in reaction to the decree of 7 May 1794 announcing a state-sanctioned belief in a benevolent deity, the so-called 'Être Suprême', and the immortality of the soul, Chénier scribbled down:

> Que croiront les mortels, quand ils verront que sous tes yeux [les yeux de l'Être Suprême] le nom de vertu est prononcé par des bouches qui..., de probité, par des bouches qui..., d'humanité, par des bouches qui..., et que tout est le sujet de leur basse et dérisoire hypocrisie...?
>
> [1] Quoi! ton œil qui voit tout, sans les réduire en cendres,
> pénètre dans les antres affreux, où les Co..., les L..., couchés sur des cadavres,
>
> [2] Rongent des ossements humains.[29]

The stand-alone alexandrine [1] and octosyllable [2] lines here, elements of incomplete iambics, are distilled or crystallized from their prose context as though the poet's thought had reached a certain critical pitch or intensity by which it suddenly alters its state, as water turns to steam or gas to crystal. The prose is not a lesser element in this exchange but a prosodic formlessness, a preliminary state that contains all the poetic forms available virtually to the poet, including those he chooses, consciously or otherwise. Chénier called these prose frames 'quadri'. Despite the clear reference to a pictorial model in this term, it is better to think of them not as large-scale framing devices borrowed from contemporary neo-classical painting, but more like varied preparatory sketches that contribute to a lyric poetry composed as a montage of phrasings and images.

★　★　★　★　★

As has often been remarked, names and naming feature prominently in Chénier's poetry and activate the performative function of language, of invocation or incantation. They don't 'mean' anything but are redolent of meaningfulness. Hailing proper names in particular reaches for the Adamic power of naming as the power to call its object into being by naming it; or conversely, to consign its object to nothingness. Whether he hails 'Fanny' or 'Marat', the poet is not naming a love-object or hate-object as she or he exists in the world prior to their naming; instead, he is conjuring into existence his object of desire or condemning to death his enemy in the very act of naming her or him. This is how both fame and infamy rest on the creative repetition of proper names, in the sense that this consolidates the good or bad public renown of their object as 're-nommée'. In deference to his classical influences, Chénier attempts in his poetry to invest eighteenth-century French with a vocative case, one that marks its object out as publicly hailed or 'interpellated', as by a friend or by the police state. Something else results from the poet's novel invocations that freely juxtapose classical gods, famous authors and revolutionary leaders, namely, a culture of celebrity as a modern polytheism.

★　★　★　★　★

Poetry is language set to work to elicit and formally (re)distribute attention and desire. Among its basic units for achieving this are the line and the stanza. Line-endings often heighten attention and desire by enjambement where the pent-up energy of one line is released in the passage to the next:

> Fanny, l'heureux mortel qui près de toi respire
> *Sait*, à te voir parler et rougir et sourire,
> De quels hôtes divins le ciel est habité. (my emphasis)

The *rejet* here (what is shunted forward by the line-break) not only resonates with the certainty of its claim to knowledge ('Sait') but it does so by closing out the breath extended by 'respire', the short vowel /ɛ/ stopping the longer exhalation of /i/ lengthened further by the *e atone*, even if this is not conventionally sounded. Rhyme is a further poetic device by which attention and/or desire is augmented at the end of a line. In the above example, Chénier doubles up on the reader's anticipation of the rhyme 'respire'/'sourire' by preceding it with the internal rhyme of 'rougir'. He pre-empts the expectancy produced by the line-end rhyme and so makes it at once more resonant and awkward (reflecting 'rougir' as an attractive natural gaucheness?). As an integral feature of classical French poetry, rhyme can also impart a sense of fatefulness to the verse, as it recurs systematically and inevitably, reverberating through the verse like so many peals of a bell. It is as though language itself had predetermined certain line-endings, thereby intensifying the sense that personal fates are likewise pre-ordained in some of Chénier's last poems.

But rhyme-schemes can also be used to modulate the larger unit of the stanza in its eliciting and (re)distribution of attention and desire in language. This is particularly the case with the skilful variations of line-lengths and rhyme-schemes that Chénier introduces in his last odes. In expanding or foreshortening the incidence of rhyme in a given stanza form, the poet plays on our attention to, and desire for, recurring homophony. He also exercises our faculty of memory and forgetting, insofar as this operates audibly, between the occurrences of rhyme. Thus, if the poem actually articulates personal memories, as does the ode 'Fanny, l'heureux mortel qui près de toi respire' cited above, the sound-memories of rhyme can ring out in order to accentuate or counter-point the life-memories evoked. In contrast, Chénier's iambics do not have a fixed stanza form but extend their a/b/a/b *rimes croisées* in a halting-hastening succession of alexandrines and octosyllables of varying length of composition. There is a decidedly tidal power to this rolling alternation of short/long line-lengths and masculine/feminine rhymes in which it is often the shorter line, appearing as a lesser force, that carries yet more devastatingly the percussive clout of the verse. As I have written elsewhere, the iambic verse-form, in its alternating line-lengths, also connotes tellingly the stark asymmetry of power between the lone poet and the Jacobin state.[30]

★ ★ ★ ★ ★

The political polarization in the Revolution is reflected in Chénier's verse by a preference for rhetorical figures that set up stark oppositions, binaries, antitheses; or that express the volatility and versatility of revolutionary political stances by figures slickly inverting their terms or doubling up on literal and figurative meanings. One such figure is the antimetabole, often seen as a subordinate form of chiasmus, in which grammatical structures are reversed while their terms are repeated: 'Et moi, *comme lui* belle, et jeune *comme lui*' ('La Jeune Captive', my emphasis), or 'Si la risée *atroce*, ou, plus *atroce* injure' ('Comme un dernier rayon', my emphasis). Another figure of this sort is the zeugma wherein a single word governs two other parts of a sentence in different ways, usually contrasting literal and figurative senses. Thus the poet's 'chisel' can engrave marble (literally) and shame (figuratively) as a doubly indelible testimony to the turpitude of his contemporaries. The poet's pen is weaponized in similar fashion: 'Dans *l'encre* et *l'amertume* une autre arme trempée | Peut encor servir les humains' ('Comme un dernier rayon', my emphasis). Whether as symmetry, inversion or as antithesis, the binary figures of Chénier's last poems leave no room for compromise, for the emergence of a median or third term. The alternating current of revolutionary power may flicker between the extreme poles of just/unjust, legal/criminal, civilized/barbarous, but as in the irreconcilable antagonism that pits Charlotte Corday against Jean-Paul Marat, it can only end in the annihilation of one or both parties.

★ ★ ★ ★ ★

Chénier's verse 'Sa langue est un fer chaud' abounds in hypallage, a rhetorical figure in which syntax is modified to link two words semantically in a misleading or inappropriate manner. The poem depicts 'doctes vallées', 'lacet vengeur' and 'pieuses morsures'. This is a form of grammatical misdirection: it is not the valleys that are learned, the noose that is avenging, or the act of biting that is pious or reverent. And yet this grammatical category error tells an atavistic truth. For the pantheist mind, a divine power pervades all matter and brings it to life in wonderful and terrifying ways. Through hypallage Chénier's late verse accedes to a primal function of poetry: to 'speak' the world as it strikes the poet in its immediacy, not as it is ordered and held at a comforting, illusory remove by reason, reflection or other forms of abstraction.

★ ★ ★ ★ ★

Poetry is language at its most primitive (poetry as 'cry') and at its most refined (poetry as 'form'). In both instances, it heightens attention in the poet (and reader) because it is not subservient to other communicative functions of language such as argument or narration. Poetry restores language to its own materiality. This is most patent in its creative use of onomatopoeia in which sound and signification are inseparable. In his 'Essai sur l'origine des langues', which first appeared posthumously in 1782, Rousseau claims that onomatopoeia were humankind's first language, produced in wondrous or worried imitation of our environment; that our first words were tropes of the natural world around us; thus 'la poésie fut trouvée avant la prose; cela devait être, puisque les passions parlèrent avant la raison' [poetry came to us before prose; this had to be, since passions spoke before reason].[31]

There are onomatopoeia in Chénier's last poems, predominantly signifying the animality to which the Terror reduces its victims: 'caquetage', 'braillent', 'bêlant'. But a similarly intrinsic meshing of sound and meaning characterizes the elemental forces that the poet asks his poetry to embody in response to the Terror: heart-beat, whip-crack, arrow-flight, chisel-strike, torch-thrust. Like the vortex of Revolution in which these sounds are emitted, their form only exists in their motion, the cry in its crying, the poetry in its declamation or reading.

In terms of the more refined formal qualities of Chénier's verse, insofar as these too restore materiality to language, we could consider the use of punctuation in his last poems. Punctuation creates its own rhythm on the page and in the mind; it imparts its own cadence to attention. On the one hand, there are the stops sounded — colon, full stop, exclamation — as so many graphic markers of brusqueness, pride, indignation, outrage. The punctuation enhances or tempers the expressions that it orchestrates. On the other, there is the weak punctuation, the asyndeta structured by comma, but especially by semi-colon, as in 'On vit; on vit infâme'. They mark the fatuity and futility of a world stripped of its reasoned and reasonable connections; an arbitrary universe in which one moment no longer relates necessarily to the next, in which actions fatally produce the wrong outcome or have little or no consequence at all.

★ ★ ★ ★ ★

Life is a cup to be drunk to the lees, a quiverful of arrows to let fly; love a sweet illusion; youth a blooming rose; poetry is sweet as honey, rich as silk, bright as pearls; the truth is gagged; lies rule; women are weak *and* seductive; politicians, snakes; tyranny, capricious; prisoners, sheep; sorrow, poison; vengeance, a whip; pride, a haughty brow; courage, fire in the veins; death, a dwelling from which one never returns but where all will follow. Chénier's poetry is not lacking in commonplaces. But we can read this not as a want of imagination or originality; rather, it is providing literal common places of language use in which the individual experiences of poet and reader meet and enrich one another. The commonplaces in Chénier's poetry then function more like dicta or proverbs: they are largely evacuated of specific meaning, and so can be deployed in diverse situations, yet they act as powerful incitations (in-citations?) to speak, to reproduce themselves, to be spoken, to be repeated, almost irrespective of context. They are more phatic than constative. They solicit citing, by poet and reader alike.

★ ★ ★ ★ ★

Lyric poetry refers originally to verse sung to the accompaniment of a lyre. So the dominant metaphor for appreciating the effects of lyric poetry is that of the string vibrating to the poet's touch and setting up a correlating emotional vibration in its listener or reader. Poetry is reverberation: both string touched and ear touched (captured in English by the homophony of 'cord' strummed and 'chord' heard). Lyric poetry is thus created between poet and listener/reader. As I have written elsewhere, Chénier gives us a fine example of this in his depiction of the primal poetic scene of Orpheus singing the world into both being and reasoned order for his fellow princes aboard the Argo. The verse fragment ends with the princes resonating with the poet's voice beyond its physical sound and so actually *creating it* themselves:

> Autour du demi-dieu les princes immobiles
> Aux accents de sa voix demeuraient suspendus,
> Et l'écoutaient encor quand il ne chantait plus.[32]

This sort of intersubjective reverberation occasioned by poetry finds expression in three principal figures: resonance, remanence, reminiscence. Yves Citton has argued convincingly that the late eighteenth-century poetic obsession with the Aeolian harp is founded on this notion of prosodic resonance.[33] The Aeolian harp is played by the wind as the poet is played by his passions, with harp and poet moving

their listeners, since their music makes a complementary emotional breeze or gale
gust through those who hear it, setting up a shared music in its audience. ('Not I,
not I but the wind that blows through me!' as D. H. Lawrence has it in his 'Song of
a Man Who has Come Through').[34] Remanence, for its part, is a figure borrowed
from magnetism describing the invisible but effective affinities set up between
magnet and iron, poet and listener, poem and reading. The shared emotional charge
in this image is made more explicit in French, since *aimant* signifies both the noun
'magnet' and the present participle or adjective 'loving', 'affectionate'. This is poetry
as emotional force field suffusing indiscriminately the individuals caught in its sway
and so dissolving their respective sense of selfhood in its words and rhythms. Yet,
of these three figures of mutually engendered affinity through poetry, it is probably
the last, reminiscence, which is most prominent in Chénier's late poems. This is
created by the contrapuntal play of absence and presence in the poet's mind and
on the page. In the odes in which 'Fanny' figures, absence becomes the condition
for the poet's momentary possession of his love-object, recalled to his mind and so
re-presented physically to him in his verse, in the interval between the last time and
the next time that he will be in her presence in the 'real' world:

> Quand, l'âme doucement émue,
> J'y viens méditer l'instant où je l'ai vue,
> Et l'instant où je dois la voir.
> ('A Versailles')

> Que, loin de moi, ton cœur fût plein de ma présence,
> Comme, dans ton absence,
> Ton aspect bien-aimé m'est présent en tous lieux!
> ('Fanny, l'heureux mortel qui près de toi respire')

In the first quotation, the *e atone*, visible but unsounded, in both 'émue' and
especially as a preceding direct object agreement in 'vue', perfectly reproduces the
interplay of absence-presence of the love-object in the poem. She can be seen as she
really is because she is not there in person. The poet can possess her (*l'avoir*) only in
his anticipation of seeing her later ('la voir'). In the second quotation, poet and lover
are brought into each other's presence in the poem, insofar as flickering images of
both are held at once in the reader's mind; a double physical 'présence' is conjured
into the here and now, the 'présent', of the reading.

Finally, I wonder if it is possible to detect a negative inflection of this evocative
power of reminiscence in Chénier's final poems. This would be expressed in the
way in which the poet's forced absence from the world (incarceration) nonetheless
allows him to take momentary possession of those who put him there (his Jacobin
enemies), as they are recalled to his mind and so re-presented to him physically in
his poetry. This possession of them would then be total, allowing the poetry to
reveal the revolutionaries' perfidy in its full horror. It would also effect a complete
reversal of the power relations between its parties: the poet now 'sees' and 'holds',
i.e. judges and detains, his gaolers:

> Ils ne sont point cachés dans leur bassesse obscure:
> Je les *vois*, j'accours, je les *tiens*.

Sur ses pieds inégaux l'épode vengeresse
Saura les atteindre pourtant.
('Ils vivent cependant et de tant de victimes', my emphasis)

★   ★   ★   ★   ★

Constantinople represents the fulcrum of cultures, of West and East, democracy and despotism, civilization and barbarism. At its heart it succeeds in reconciling these apparent opposites, turning their creative tensions to fruitful production, as it does in Candide's 'garden', which is at once nature and culture. This is the polyglot birthplace of André Chénier and, allegedly, the polyglot birthplace of comparative literature in the 1930s.[35] It is the real and imaginary space of a transnational humanism.

★   ★   ★   ★   ★

Chénier's last poems clearly subvert the bucolic genre. The figure of the shepherd-poet of his Arcadian idylls is incarcerated in the Terror, becoming the poet-sheep, penned for imminent slaughter. This is a powerful critique of the denaturing effect of Jacobin rule and its barbaric inversion of a seemingly 'natural' order. But perhaps Chénier also denounces here the unnaturalness of the pastoral myth itself; the fact that pastoralism effaces real-world power struggles beneath a veneer of rustic peace and an illusory communion with nature. Revolutionaries enthusiastically adapted the same pastoral myth to their own political ends, from planting liberty trees to imposing the thoroughly bucolic revolutionary calendar. The Revolution itself was frequently portrayed as a glorious 'dawn' or the 'springtime' of humanity. Yet in doing so, the revolutionaries ultimately exposed the workings of the same pastoral mythologizing: the profound unnaturalness of a permanent dawn or an eternal spring. Pastoralism as an idyll of timeless natural concord does not signify the absence of conflict so much as present the preferred story that a hegemonic power tells itself, a story of 'natural' order that it imposes on those it relentlessly crushes. This is just as true for the Revolution as it is for the *Ancien Régime*. If we read again, then, the hugely popular bucolic poems of Roucher and Delille, *Les Mois* (1779) and *Les Jardins* (1780) respectively, their neat and regular alexandrine couplets paint a picture of the sempiternally rolling harmonies of nature. It took Erasmus Darwin's scandalous *The Loves of the Plants* (1789), a poetic setting of Linnaeus's highly sexualized explanation of plant reproduction, to show that the bucolic world epitomized by flora was actually one of subtle and brutal power struggles. Darwin's heroic couplets, organized in four cantos like Delille's *Jardins*, are in effect compulsive couplings, the promiscuous reality of the sex life of plants (and, by implication, the power-vexed and desire-ridden reality of all living beings, including humans).

★   ★   ★   ★   ★

André Chénier began as a precocious translator-poet among a generation of poet-translators. In 1769 the poet Jacques Delille made his name with a translation of

Virgil's *Georgics*. The following year Charles-Pierre Colardeau published a verse translation of the first two 'nights' of Edward Young's influential *Night-Thoughts*. Through the 1770s Michel-Paul Gui de Chabanon brought out widely-read translations of Pindar and Theocritus. Among his contemporaries, Chénier's school friend Michel Trudaine translated texts from the American insurgents and Jean-Antoine Roucher published a translation of Adam Smith's *Inquiry into the Nature and Causes of the Wealth of Nations* in 1790 (he was revising the second edition of this text when he was called away to step into the tumbril with Chénier in July 1794). Translation from Greek and Latin classics was a staple of late eighteenth-century schooling. So there is nothing unusual about the adolescent Chénier cutting his poetic teeth on translations of Homer, Virgil, Sappho, etc. However, as this developed into a more sustained poetic practice for him, it became less about re-writing Greek than it was about re-wiring French. The most accomplished of the poet's early translations, as Jean Fabre has remarked, were not meek copies but bold creations.[36] They didn't so much rework their source texts as undo them via the medium of French. Conversely, the impact on Chénier's French verse was to 'foreignize' it. In a sense, this was only following Aristotle's counsel in his *Poetics* — incidentally, a text that the poet's younger brother Marie-Joseph would translate — that poetry should read like a foreign language.[37] The foreignness was most pronounced in the syntax. Chénier sought to inflect French as though it were a case language like Greek or Latin; one might say, he sought to speak his mother tongue (French) with his mother's tongue (a Greek living in Constantinople). The effect, especially through inversions, is to bend the grammatical order to express the affective order of the poet's thoughts and feelings. Further foreignizing influences followed — Italian, English, Persian, Arabic — whether mastered fluently, experienced immersively, studied remotely, half-learnt, or conflated partly with each other. In the fragments that Chénier left for an extended essay on the history of western literature, he claims that a poet, mastering a language such as French in all its intrinsic richness, must not be afraid to:

> Lui faire [à la langue française] une heureuse violence pour qu'elle s'attache après une langue étrangère, et lui ravisse quelque tournure forte et originale qui l'effarouche d'abord, mais que l'habitude lui fera bientôt aimer.[38]

That is, translated roughly, 'the poet should inflict a benign violence on French so that it accommodates original and powerful turns of phrase from foreign tongues, turns of phrase that might shock the ear initially but which the French language itself will come to cherish'. This muscular polyglot enrichment of French then stands in opposition to the state-sponsored revolutionary monolingualism that was rolled out across France in 1794 with the express aim of 'annihilating' patois, i.e. diverse regional languages, and 'universalizing' the use of a 'one and indivisible' French idiom made in the image of the Jacobin state.[39]

★   ★   ★   ★   ★

Translation

In school and university classrooms, translations are often assessed by a notion of how 'near to', or how 'far from', the source text they appear to be. This derives from an older sense of translation signifying the transporting of an object from one place to another. This sense is attested in eighteenth-century French dictionaries in which the very term *translation* means 'Transport, action par laquelle on fait passer une chose d'un lieu à un autre' [Transport, action by which one moves an object from one place to another].[40] Hence textual translation is the transporting of meaning from one language to another and from one document to another. The measure of a more effective translation thus becomes the shorter 'distance' covered between words or expressions, a mark of how 'closely' the translation holds to the 'original'. This is translation conceived of as a form of linguistic transfer or extension across languages. However, eighteenth-century French dictionaries also indicate that there is a secondary sense to *transport* that modifies how we might understand translation too. *Transport* has a widely used figurative and literary meaning as the occurrence of violent passions 'qui nous mettent en quelque sorte hors de nous-mêmes'.[41] This kind of *transport* doesn't move us from one place to another, it moves us emotionally; it is exaltation not displacement, it is self-estranging intensity not self-affirming extension. What if we then consider translation in the light of this alternative meaning of transport? It would no longer be about a textual transfer of meaning across languages, but the creation of a powerful mood, a singular atmosphere, that would allow the reader to inhabit to a weaker or stronger degree the affective environment of the source text in the very act of reading the target text. Translation would be a means of bringing both the source text and the reader to a state 'hors d'eux-mêmes', beside themselves emotionally, not spatially.

For Chénier, angry and imprisoned, there can clearly be no other physical 'transport' than an emotional one. Thus he apostrophizes his own intense feelings of bitterness and resentment as a paradoxical source of hope keeping him alive:

> Je souffre; mais je vis. Par vous, loin de mes peines,
> D'espérance un vaste torrent
> *Me transporte.*
> ('Comme un dernier rayon', my emphasis)

A translation of these iambics could then attempt to generate a correlative intensity of passion in language, not a conveyance of meaning that sticks 'closely' to the 'original'.

★ ★ ★ ★ ★

What I've learnt: in front of my open copy of André Chénier's *Œuvres complètes*, translation starts from not knowing. And as it is practised, it deepens this initial realization, and becomes a profound awareness of never knowing enough — enough about André Chénier, the French Revolution, the French language, the English language, and so on and so forth. What remains is translation as a reading activity, a particular form of attention to the text, available to anyone, albeit in different ways. Translating then becomes what Kate Briggs calls 'a scene of learning'.[42] And it starts to offer up an alternative form of knowledge: not what the source text means, but how it works. It works differently; each poem, each line works differently. So translating each poem, each line differs each time we return to the text. The little knowledge gleaned from translating then includes the appreciation that no single translation methodology can address the diverse ways in which the source text works. Hence the variety of approaches adopted here. Applying myself daily to translating the last poems of André Chénier, I've learnt that translation doesn't have an object as such, but is an exercise, a series of micro-events, a scene rehearsed over and over again, differing slightly each time. The source text doesn't give me any answers but it teaches me to question it more attentively each time I return to it.

Oddly enough, a similar misapprehension about knowledge formation lay behind the failure of Chénier's great philosophical-poetic projects, 'Hermès' and 'L'Amérique'. Despite, or because of, his prodigious poetic gifts, Chénier forgot that poetry constitutes a discrete, alternative means of knowing the world and so his own poetry was fatally vitiated when this distinct appreciation of the world was subordinated to *la philosophie*, reduced to the role of a rhyming vehicle for a positivist exposition of Western 'progress'.[43]

As in poetry, there's no progress in translation. We don't read or translate 'better' than the ancient Greeks or eighteenth-century Europeans did. We just read and translate differently. This lack of progress might seem disheartening, but it isn't. Get used to it. Open the book again, translate some more. Exercise your ignorance.

★   ★   ★   ★   ★

If we take one — any one — of these translations of Chénier's last poems, it allows its poem to express something that the French poem has not hitherto expressed and that it was unaware that it could ever express in this form. The translation actualizes in the target text one of the source text's polyphonic voices; but this is never just a localized operation from a source text to a target text. It is more exactly a translation with the source text and the target text, as a particular staging of the interaction between two language systems. New interpretive possibilities are opened up not just in the texts but also in the source and target languages. The translation makes a new voice in the target language, exercising the linguistic and phonic resources of that language as though it were being acquired for the first time by a language learner.[44] Something of this conception of the translation process is articulated in one of Chénier's last poems, the poignant 'Sur la mort d'un enfant'. In the poem we hear the lost accents of the child being mourned:

> Nous ne recevrons plus, avec des cris joyeux,
> Les efforts impuissants de ta bouche vermeille
> A bégayer les sons offerts à ton oreille.

The physicality of trying out new sounds is rendered in the stammering of 'bégayer', but this is also a synaesthetic experience, since we 'see' at the same time the ruby colour of the child's mouth, her 'bouche vermeille', opening and closing round its half-formed words.[45] So Chénier translates the child's prattling into verse, but not just into words that now make sense, he also evokes senses (sound, colour) that make words. The poem circulates sounds: the 'sons offerts' to the child's ear prompt her attempted mimicking of them, 'bégayer', which prompt the 'cris joyeux' of the adults who hear her jabbering. These last cries are presumably further sounds that the child can try to reproduce (hence the inverted sequence of sounds in the poems: adult cries first, then stammering, then sounds heard — unless this represents instead the play-back order of the poet's memory?). The translation of this poem then partakes of the physicality and the circularity of the source text's sound-production. Child babble ↔ poetic babble ↔ translation babble. The translation makes available the *energeia* or potential of meaning-making of Chénier's verse for its reader, just as Chénier's verse makes available the *energeia* or potential of meaning-making of the child's half-articulated speech. These childish noises, then, are ultimately not 'efforts impuissants', since they provoke the double response of 'cris joyeux' and the poem relating them; rather, they are meanings *en puissance*, awaiting their actualization in verse and translation.

★   ★   ★   ★   ★

As Clive Scott argues, some prevailing models of translation practice are flawed in that they implicitly presume the reader to be an Anglophone monoglot.[46] Hence a conceptualization of translating that is based on notions of equivalence, reliability or fidelity obtaining exclusively between two semi-closed language systems, e.g. French and English. This is a false conceptualization on a number of levels. (For starters, even the Anglophone monoglot is likely to speak a patois with friends or children, let alone mastering diverse registers to communicate with public authorities, bosses, elderly neighbours, lovers, pals, etc., via letter, conversation, email, text message, Twitter, and the like.) Instead, Scott maintains, translation should be conceived of as a naturally occurring polyglot practice.

André Chénier spoke several languages, ancient and modern, some more fluently than others. His multilingualism clearly informs his poetry, if only in his Latinate lexis and syntax. He was also a practising translator both from and into Latin and Greek and we have samples of his philological notes on these languages as well as on Chinese literature.[47] As far as my own translations are concerned, they are clearly informed by my proficiency in English and French, but also by my working knowledge of a couple of other European languages. While some translations might seem to tend towards a monoglot model of equivalence between the French and English texts, this is a superficial and deceptive reading of them. Consciously or otherwise, they have been produced in a multilingual matrix of ideas, feelings and expressions. To give just one example of how a multilingual reading could — but does not have to — inform the translation process, let us look again at one of the more vernacular terms that Chénier introduces into his iambics:

> Quel remords agite le flanc,
> Tourmente le sommeil du [tribunal] impie
> Qui mange, boit, *rote* du sang?

As an English-speaker, the translator might read 'rot' into 'rote' here, and so try to evoke the stinking moral corruption of the revolutionary officials in Nantes or, more materially, the stench of the dead flesh that they ingest. However, if the translator is a German-speaker, he or she will be predisposed to read into 'rote' the colour red, *rot(e)*, thereby intensifying the sensation of blood flowing thickly or brightly and drunk like wine (also collocated with *rot*/'red').

As it stands, my own translation of this poem is among the more experimental in this edition. So it forgoes either of these translation possibilities involving the more obvious English and German lexes as intensifiers of corruption or redness. Instead, it renders the passage cited above as:

> But what remorse eats
> At the liver pollutes the sleep of these
> Troughers of blood.

By modulating its terms, this translation introduces active allusions to consumption (eats) and corruption (pollutes) at an earlier point in the poem. It also replicates the sharp [i] sounds of the source text's 'agite', 'impie, | Qui' in the words 'eats', 'sleep', 'these', as so many shrill notes of conscience that repeatedly fail to move the murderous Jacobins. The line-lengths similarly retain the see-sawing alternation of Chénier's iambics, albeit without the precise syllable count of the French text. The longer line-break falls on the unstressed demonstrative 'these' as a means of accentuating the poet's aim of holding up precisely *these* monstrous individuals to public opprobrium. This sense of horrified dismay is further underlined in the English by a lack of punctuation that obliges the reader to weigh each word successively not just for its semantic but also for its syntactical signification. Finally, the line 'Qui mange, boit, rote du sang' is reworked as 'Troughers of blood', a translation which keeps a familiar register in the term 'troughers', rendering, too, a sense of pig-snouts snuffling in a pail, as a means of emphasizing the revolutionaries' greed and animality. This four-syllable line provides an echo to the earlier line 'Bayers of blood' referring to the Jacobin-selected judges and juries whose only role was to serially sentence the accused to death, so that 'baying' and 'troughing' overlay animal noise and appetite in order to make the revolutionaries' bloodthirstiness both audible and visceral for the reader.

★ ★ ★ ★ ★

Translation is a tightrope walk between hubris and humility.

★ ★ ★ ★ ★

Rhyme is a major device for (re)distributing attention and desire in language, as it provides stylized points of both expectation and satisfaction at the line-breaks or, more rarely, internally to the verse. The same is true of rhyme's function in translation. However, the received wisdom is that English, as a syllable-and-stress poetic language, with a celebrated tradition of blank verse, is less reliant than French on the prosodic efficacy of rhyme. I don't know how far this wisdom still holds.

But what seems more certain is that *rime riche* especially in English today can feel sickly sweet, a surfeit of homophony, not a knowing modulation of like sounds, and so tends to be deployed for ironic, comic, even bathetic effect.[48] The approach to rhyming then in these translations of Chénier's last poems — all of which use strong rhyme-schemes — has been to graduate the incidence and intensity of rhyme in the target texts. Thus, on occasion, the rhyme-scheme corresponds more or less fully to the source text, as in 'La Jeune Captive', in which the completeness of rhyme is intended to relay some of the wide-eyed naivety of the young woman's thoughts, as these are presented with a certain irony by the poet interpreting their shared fate. In the ode 'A Byzance', complete rhymes in English are predominantly retained but the rhyme-scheme is modified from the source text's *rimes croisées* to one of *rimes embrassées*. This latter *abba* rhyme-scheme in translation produces enclosed quatrains that reflect the poem's preoccupation with contrasting forms of confinement: the peaceful Turk's house and the pleasures of the harem that are untroubled by the abusive intrusions of state officials into private homes, leading to arbitrary arrest and imprisonment. The containment of the enveloping *a*-rhymes replicates that of sharia law reining in any temptation the Sultan might feel to exercise despotism, so that an Eastern form of legal restraint allows for a modicum of civil liberty, something now wholly denied to the French under the Terror. Elsewhere, especially in the iambics, the translations loosen the rhymes, even where they broadly respect the rhyme-scheme. So the stress of the rhyme might fall regularly only on the shorter lines, giving greater scope in the longer lines to develop ideas, imagery or cultivate soundscapes. Rhymes in many of the translations of the iambics are half-rhymes, since their dissonance often captures well the poet's dissidence. The principal exception to this practice among the iambics is the translation of 'Comme un dernier rayon'. What I have tried to do in translating this poem is to produce the richest rhymes possible in rendering the alexandrines of the source text, a rhyme so complete that it becomes a sort of anti-rhyme (akin in this regard to Chénier's own nonsense-rhyming of proper names). These rich rhymes are meant to ring hollowly with the lucid disillusion that is maintained throughout the poem, even as it swings emotionally from despair to defiance, from resignation to rage.

★   ★   ★   ★   ★

Chénier would appreciate the translation scholar's expression of 'source text'. He would welcome the richness of the word 'source', resonant in French with 'well-spring', and so constituting as much an endless flow without beginning or end as a specific origin. Hence the multiple rivers, from the ancient Alpheus and Cocytus to the contemporary Seine and Loire, that rise, fall, meander and flow out of and into his poetry.[49]

★   ★   ★   ★   ★

Poetic genres are important to Chénier as one of the 'bonds that free', the constraints that are a precondition for fully realizing a poetic freedom of expression. Yet *genre* in French signifies both 'genre' and 'gender' in English. The poet's sensitivity to generic forms in his verse extends to an embodied and linguistic appreciation of gender too. It encompasses diverse aspects of republican homosociability, from the revolutionaries' self-conception as a warrior brotherhood to classical love between men, as in his reference in the ode 'A Marie-Anne-Charlotte Corday' to Harmodius and his 'ami', that is, his lover Aristogeiton. What connects both of these instances is a homosociability that finds its ultimate expression not in platonic or carnal love but in homicide. Chénier's ode to Marat's murderess is his most explicit and vexed articulation of contemporary gender norms. Charlotte Corday's cold-blooded, premeditated assassination of the journalist-*député* is understood as the assumption of a wholly masculine virility that throws into stark relief the impotent effeminacy of her male contemporaries. The sexual binary (male/female) is inverted through gendered performance (feminine/masculine) while maintaining a strict sense of intractable antithesis between its terms. This is brilliantly expressed in a single hemistich: 'Seule tu fus un homme'. It also demonstrates the poetic resources of a gendered language that can create this jarring clash between the feminine adjective ('seule') and the masculine predicate ('homme'). This particular effect is unavailable in English. What is more, rhymes are also construed as gendered in French, with 'feminine' rhymes ending on an unaccentuated *e atone* while all 'masculine' rhymes do not. In classical poetics, to avoid the monotony of unrelieved accentuation in rhyming, masculine and feminine rhymes always alternate. If this represents a strange form of linguistic gender equality not evident elsewhere in early modern society, I have attempted a very occasional twenty-first-century corrective to this situation in translating some epicene (i.e. gender-neutral) nouns as feminine. For instance, the 'antique athlète' of the Pindaric ode 'O mon esprit, au sein des cieux', inferred as masculine in French, is rendered in translation as the 'true athlete' holding 'herself' 'unmoved | And unmoveable' while trash, both material and social, swirls about 'her feet'.

★   ★   ★   ★   ★

André Chénier's first published revolutionary iambics, the 'Hymne sur l'entrée triomphale des Suisses révoltés du régiment de Châteauvieux', were inspired by a grotesque abuse of the law, as the poet saw it. The procession celebrating the amnesty granted to the Swiss mutineers was not a public manifestation of revolutionary progress as Chénier understood it, but a regressive, populist parade, a carnival in which the legal order was turned on its head. It thus represented a literal miscarriage of justice. Thus, when the revolutionary authorities prove incapable of delivering justice, it becomes the business of the poet to do so. Chénier might then be seen to anticipate and incarnate Shelley's famous conclusion to his *Defence of Poetry* (1821) that 'poets are the unacknowledged legislators of the world'.[50]

   This is relevant to translation because the expression in French 'to bring someone to justice', to arraign someone physically before the courts, is *traduire quelqu'un en justice*. This understanding of *traduire* clearly harks back to the spatial meaning of translation as transporting an object from one place to another. Yet, with a bit of poetic licence, we might extend this French collocation of 'translation' and 'justice' to infer that it should also be the business of a translation itself to 'do justice' to its source text in the same way that the poet sought to 'do justice' to his vision of the Revolution in his 'Hymne'. Such a conception of translating makes it a form of advocacy, as it pleads the case for its source text before its reader. 'Getting justice' for its literary source text suggests too that a translation should go beyond mere equivalences in syntax and lexis. Fairness is a sort of transcendent concept here that means more than any academic 'fair' copy can provide, in the same way that justice means more than *justesse* or a particular correctness in judgement. Translation has a significant performative value, not an axiomatic one. It takes its lead from legislation as Montaigne practised and presented it, that is, as the most persuasive expression of legality, with no inherent justness in it other than the one realized as its speech 'enacts' the rule of law.[51] So the target text 'does' justice to the source text by affording its reader the most effective performative interpretation of it.

★ ★ ★ ★ ★

No matter how brief the interval between the publication and reading of the source text and its translation, the translator necessarily engages with language and text anachronistically. It is precisely in this temporal disjunction between reading the source text and reading the target text that language is heard afresh, new feelings sensed, alternative meanings made. Translation as anachrony foregrounds the experiential time of reading over the literary-historical time in which the source text is often embedded. This is how Chénier appears to read and translate classical Greek and Latin texts in late eighteenth-century France; he reads and translates them as urgent contemporary works, not as literary-historical documents. This is not the simple act of updating the translator's source texts, it is their 'un-dating'. They are liberated from the temporal straitjacket of conventional literary history in which a source text is fetishized as a relatively 'original' work located in a one-way current of earlier influences on it (upstream) and the inspiration it affords later works (downstream). One of the strangest things about a translation privileging the place and moment of its own reading is that it can flip this historical determinism completely. So one can find traces of Proust in Laclos or see clearly that Chénier had read his Wordsworth.[52] It is also the reason why I felt I could translate the following from 'O mon esprit, au sein des cieux':

> Mais si Mars est pour eux, leurs vertus, leurs bienfaits,
> Sont bénis de la terre entière.
> Tout s'obscurcit auprès de la splendeur guerrière;
> Elle éblouit les yeux, et sur les noirs forfaits
> Étend un voile de lumière.

as:

> Is it not the case that whoever has the guns has the glory?
> Light glancing off epaulettes, helmets and light
> Weaponry is not without aesthetic effect.
> The vapour trails hatched by their whooshing jets demarcate
> A dazing white no-fly zone over the truth.

The anachronisms here make sense much more than would a translation of this passage wedded to Greek gods or figures of French enlightenment/obscurantism. As Clive Scott writes: 'translation is not about the preservation of a text, but about the projection of a text into its possible futures'.[53]

Notes to the Introduction

1. George Gordon Noel, Lord Byron, *Byron's Letters and Journals*, ed. by Leslie A. Marchand, 13 vols (London: John Murray, 1973–94), VIII, 47.

2. André Chénier, 'Procès-verbal de l'interrogatoire d'André Chénier', in *Œuvres en prose*, ed. by Louis Moland (Paris: Garnier Frères, 1879), pp. xi–xvi. Unless stated otherwise, all translations are my own.

3. Romer braids the iambics of 'Quand au mouton bêlant' and 'Comme un dernier rayon' in this translation. See *French Poetry: From Medieval to Modern Times*, ed. by Patrick McGuinness (New York, London, & Toronto: Alfred A. Knopf, 2017), pp. 59–60.

4. <https://commons.wikimedia.org/wiki/Category:Portraits_of_Andr%C3%A9_Ch%C3%A9nier#/media/File:Andr%C3%A9_Ch%C3%A9nier_(by_Joseph-Beno%C3%AEt_Suv%C3%A9e).jpg> [accessed 15 May 2020].

5. Chénier, 'Écrou du 19 ventôse no. 787', in *Œuvres en prose*, p. xvii.

6. Catriona Seth, '"Inscrire sa mémoire aux fastes d'Hélicon": poéthique d'André Chénier', in *Revue d'histoire littéraire de la France*, 119.4 (2019), 801–20 (p. 816); and Anne Coudreuse, 'Élégie, souffle historique et pathétique dans la poésie d'André Chénier', in *Babel: Littératures plurielles*, 12 (2005), 79–90.

7. Translations of the verse appear in the next section of the book so they are not repeated in the Introduction.

8. Camille Desmoulins, letter to his father on the first anniversary of the fall of the monarchy, 10 August 1793. Cited in Marisa Linton, *Choosing Terror: Virtue, Friendship, and Authenticity in the French Revolution* (Oxford: Oxford University Press, 2013), p. 202.

9. See *Anthologie de la poésie française XVIIIe siècle, XIXe siècle, XXe siècle*, ed. by Martine Bercot, Michel Collot and Catriona Seth (Paris: Gallimard, 2000), p. 391.

10. In principle, there were twelve members of the Committee. But the twelfth, Marie-Jean Hérault de Séchelles, was suspected of collusion with foreign agents and mistrusted because of his noble background, so he was largely kept at a remove from the Committee's work. Embroiled in financial scandals in early 1794, he went to the guillotine with the Dantonists on 5 April 1794. Strangely enough, Hérault de Séchelles appears to have been an object of suspicion and scorn for Chénier too. See *Œuvres complètes*, p. 572.

11. R. R. Palmer, *Twelve Who Ruled: The Year of the Terror in the French Revolution* (Princeton, NJ: Princeton University Press, 1941); Marc Bouloiseau, *Le Comité de Salut Public* (Paris: Presses universitaires de France, 1962).

12. Sophie Wahnich, *La Liberté ou la mort: essai sur la Terreur et le terrorisme* (Paris: La Fabrique, 2003).

13. Bouloiseau, *Le Comité de Salut Public*, p. 126.

14. Daniel Arasse, *La Guillotine et l'imaginaire de la Terreur* (Paris: Flammarion, 1987), pp. 170–75.

15. Jean Fabre, *Chénier* (Paris: Hatier, 1965), p. 51.

16. Linton, *Choosing Terror*, pp. 217, 223.

17. André Chénier, *Œuvres poétiques*, ed. by Georges Buisson and Édouard Guitton, 2 vols (Orléans: Paradigme, 2005–10), I, 62–63.

18. Chénier, *Œuvres en prose*, pp. l–li.

19. André Chénier, *Poems*, ed. by Francis Scarfe (Oxford: Basil Blackwell, 1961), p. xxiii.

20. Pierre Albert-Birot, cited in Christine Lombez, 'Avec qui traduit-on? Les imaginaires de la traduction poétique', *Itinéraires*, 2018.2–3 (2019) <https://journals.openedition.org/itineraires/4561> [accessed 15 May 2020].

21. Fabre, *Chénier*, p. 121.

22. André Chénier, *Œuvres complètes*, ed. by Gérard Walter (Paris: Gallimard, 1950), pp. 891–92.

23. Ibid., p. 126.
24. William Wordsworth, *Lyrical Ballads, with Pastoral and Other Poems*, 2nd edn, 2 vols (London: T. N. Longman and O. Rees, 1802), I, xxxvii–xxxviii.
25. Chénier, *Œuvres complètes*, p. 569.
26. On the contemporary notion of 'zeitgeist', see Maike Oergel, *Zeitgeist — How Ideas Travel: Politics, Culture and the Public in the Age of Revolution* (Berlin: De Gruyter, 2019).
27. Jean-François Marmontel, cited in Jean M. Goulemot and Jean-Jacques Tatin-Gourier, *André Chénier: poésie et politique* (Paris: Minerve, 2005), p. 112.
28. Fabre, *Chénier*, pp. 148–50.
29. Chénier, *Œuvres complètes*, p. 570. 'What will mortals believe when they see that before your eyes [the eyes of the Supreme Being] the name of virtue is pronounced by mouths that..., the term integrity by mouths that..., the term humanity by mouths that..., and that everything is subject to their base and derisive hypocrisy? | What! your eye that sees all, without reducing them to ashes | pierces their horrid lairs where the likes of Co... and L..., seated on corpses | Gnaw on human remains.'
30. David McCallam, 'André Chénier's "dernières poésies": Animism and the Terror', *Forum for Modern Languages Studies*, 51.3 (July 2015), 304–15.
31. Jean-Jacques Rousseau, 'Essai sur l'origine des langues', in *Œuvres complètes de Jean-Jacques Rousseau*, 13 vols (Paris: Hachette, 1905), I, 370–408.
32. David McCallam, 'Orphée ou la poésie incarnée chez André Chénier', *Revue des littératures et des arts*, 17 (Autumn 2017) <https://revues.univ-pau.fr/opcit/278> [accessed 16 May 2020]. 'Around the demigod, the motionless princes | Hung on the sound and cadence of his voice | Listening to him still when he no longer sang.'
33. Yves Citton, 'Imitation inventrice et harpe éolienne chez André Chénier: une théorisation de la productivité par l'Ailleurs', in *Ferments d'Ailleurs: transferts culturels entre Lumières et romantismes*, ed. by D. Bonnecase and F. Genton (Grenoble: ELLUG, 2010), pp. 35–77.
34. D. H. Lawrence, *The Complete Poems* (Ware: Wordsworth Editions, 1994), p. 195.
35. Emily Apter, *The Translation Zone: A New Comparative Literature* (Princeton, NJ: Princeton University Press, 2006), pp. 41–64.
36. Fabre, *Chénier*, pp. 180–81, 186–87.
37. Ibid., p. 160.
38. Chénier, *Œuvres complètes*, p. 687.
39. See abbé Henri Grégoire, 'Rapport sur la nécessité et les moyens d'anéantir les patois, et d'universaliser l'usage de la langue française', presented to the Convention Nationale, 4 June 1794. <https://fr.wikisource.org/wiki/Rapport_sur_la_n%C3%A9cessit%C3%A9_et_les_moyens_d%E2%80%99an%C3%A9antir_les_patois_et_d%E2%80%99universaliser_l%E2%80%99usage_de_la_langue_fran%C3%A7aise> [accessed 29 November 2020].
40. For instance, *Dictionnaire de l'Académie française*, 5th edn, 2 vols (Paris: Smits et Cie, 1798), II, 694.
41. Ibid.
42. Kate Briggs, *This Little Art* (London: Fitzcarraldo, 2017), p. 165.
43. Fabre, *Chénier*, p. 230.
44. Clive Scott, *The Work of Literary Translation* (Cambridge: Cambridge University Press, 2018), p. 36.
45. Even though the poem genders the child as male (perhaps for reasons of poetic euphony?), the verse was written about Mme Lecouteulx's first daughter, Charlotte, who died in early 1792. See Francis Scarfe, *André Chénier: His Life and Work, 1762–1794* (Oxford: Clarendon Press, 1965), p. 293; see also Scarfe's notes in Chénier, *Poems*, p. 138.
46. Scott, *The Work of Literary Translation*, pp. 2–8.
47. Chénier, *Œuvres complètes*, pp. 616–19, 759–79.
48. Clive Scott, *French Verse-art: A Study* (Cambridge: Cambridge University Press, 1980), pp. 104–06.
49. On Chénier and the poetics of water, see Gérard Lahouati, 'Un pèlerinage aux sources: éléments pour une poétique de l'eau chez André Chénier', in *Lectures d'André Chénier: Imitations et préludes poétiques, Art d'aimer, Élégies*, ed. by Jean-Noël Pascal (Rennes: Presses universitaires de Rennes, 2005), pp. 61–80.

50. Percy Bysshe Shelley, *A Defence of Poetry*, in *Shelley's Poetry and Prose*, ed. by Donald H. Reiman and Neil Fraistat, 2nd edn (New York & London: Norton, 2002), p. 535. For the importance of this conception of the poet in France after Chénier, see Roger Pearson's magisterial *Unacknowledged Legislators: The Poet as Lawgiver in Post-revolutionary France* (Oxford: Oxford University Press, 2016).
51. Michel de Montaigne, *Essais*, ed. by P. Villey and V. L. Saulnier, 3 vols (Paris: Presses universitaires de France, 1965), III, 474–75.
52. Henri Duranton, 'Laclos a-t-il lu Proust?', in *Le Siècle de Voltaire: hommage à René Pomeau*, ed. by Christiane Mervaud and Sylvain Menant, 2 vols (Oxford: Voltaire Foundation, 1987), I, 449–56.
53. Scott, *The Work of Literary Translation*, p. 109.

POÉSIES

~

POEMS

Hymne sur l'entrée triomphale des Suisses révoltés du régiment de
Châteauvieux, fêtés à Paris sur une motion de Collot-d'Herbois[1]

Salut, divin Triomphe! entre dans nos murailles!
  Rends-nous ces guerriers illustrés
Par le sang de Désille, et par les funérailles
  De tant de Français massacrés.
Jamais rien de si grand n'embellit ton entrée,
  Ni quand l'ombre de Mirabeau
S'achemina jadis vers la voûte sacrée
  Où la gloire donne un tombeau,
Ni quand Voltaire mort, et sa cendre bannie
  Rentrèrent aux murs de Paris,
Vainqueurs du fanatisme et de la calomnie,
  Prosternés devant ses écrits.
Un seul jour peut atteindre à tant de renommée,
  Et ce beau jour luira bientôt!
C'est quand tu conduiras Jourdan à notre armée,
  Et Lafayette à l'échafaud.
Quelle rage à Coblentz! quel deuil pour tous ces princes,
  Qui, partout diffamant nos lois,
Excitent contre nous et contre nos provinces
  Et les esclaves et les rois!
Ils voudraient nous voir tous à la folie en proie.
  Que leur front doit être abattu!
Tandis que parmi nous quel orgueil, quelle joie,
  Pour les amis de la vertu!
Pour vous tous, ô mortels, qui rougissez encore,
  Et qui savez baisser les yeux!
De voir des échevins, que la Râpée honore,
  Asseoir sur un char radieux
Ces héros, que jadis sur les bancs des galères
  Assit un arrêt outrageant,
Et qui n'ont égorgé que très peu de nos frères,
  Et volé que très peu d'argent.
Eh bien, que tardez-vous, harmonieux Orphées?
  Si sur la tombe des Persans
Jadis Pindare, Eschyle, ont dressé des trophées;
  Il faut de plus nobles accents.
Quarante meurtriers, chéris de Robespierre,
  Vont s'élever sur nos autels.
Beaux-arts, qui faites vivre et la toile et la pierre,
  Hâtez-vous, rendez immortels
Le grand Collot-d'Herbois, ses clients helvétiques,
  Ce front que donne à des héros

Anthem for the Swiss Mutineers of the
Châteauvieux Regiment

A magnificent parade is coming to town!
A tickertape triumph through the streets
For warriors who bloodied the white flag of truce
And then slit our citizens' throats.
We've not seen its like before. Not Mirabeau's
Doleful hearse that transported him
To glory beneath the Pantheon's dome
Nor the common acclamation
That greeted the return of Voltaire's ashes,
Banished before but now recalled
To remind us how wit fillets fanatics
And puts hypocrites to the sword.
Can just one day then outdo so much fame?
And can such a day be now at hand!
To see Lafayette dance from the gallows
And bloodthirsty Jourdan command
Our armies? Our enemies must be fuming!
How they'll regret those days
When they were able to arm against us
A motley of tyrants and slaves.
They longed for us to fall prey to madness —
How they must be gnawing their fists
Since crowds here erupt in noisy rejoicing
And true patriots line the streets!
And you, there, understandably confounded,
Blushing, unsure where to look,
See your proud aldermen, flush from a spree,
Give their heroes a short leg-up
Onto bandwagons with much plusher seating
Than they got in the galley pews
Where they'd laboured under the misunderstanding
Of having gunned down — at most a few —
Blameless souls, then made off with the petty cash.
But new heroes need new bards
To out-croon the old ones with their epic voices,
Their flowing beards and soaring harps.
Here forty murderers whom Robespierre loves
Will pose on the city-hall steps
So, sculptors, artists, photographers,
Time for you to rise to the test
And capture for posterity the great
Collot and his Swiss mercenaries

La vertu, la taverne, et le secours des piques,
    Peuplez le ciel d'astres nouveaux,
O vous, enfants d'Eudoxe et d'Hipparque et d'Euclide.
    C'est par vous que les blonds cheveux
Qui tombèrent du front d'une reine timide,
    Sont tressés en célestes feux.
Par vous l'heureux vaisseau des premiers Argonautes
    Flotte encor dans l'azur des airs.
Faites gémir Atlas sous de plus nobles hôtes,
    Comme eux dominateurs des mers.
Que la Nuit de leurs noms embellisse ses voiles,
    Et que le nocher aux abois
Invoque en leur Galère, ornement des étoiles,
    Les Suisses de Collot-d'Herbois.

'Sa langue est un fer chaud'[2]

'Sa langue est un fer chaud. Dans ses veines brûlées
    Serpentent des fleuves de fiel.'
J'ai douze ans en secret dans les doctes vallées
    Cueilli le poétique miel.
Je veux un jour ouvrir ma ruche tout entière;
    Dans tous mes vers on pourra voir
Si ma Muse naquit haineuse et meurtrière.
    Frustré d'un amoureux espoir,
Archiloque aux fureurs du belliqueux ïambe
    Immole un beau-père menteur.
Moi, ce n'est point au col d'un perfide Lycambe
    Que j'apprête un lacet vengeur.
Ma foudre n'a jamais tonné pour mes injures.
    La patrie allume ma voix;
La paix seule aguerrit mes pieuses morsures;
    Et mes fureurs servent les lois.
Contre les noirs Pythons et les hydres fangeuses
    Le feu, le fer arment mes mains;
Extirper sans pitié les bêtes venimeuses,
    C'est donner la vie aux humains.

Ennobled by virtue of booze and thugs —
Do more than just show them to us:
Set them in their own new constellation,
A blaze of musket-fire on high,
So we can chart our courses by them, outshining
Leo, Boötes and the Plough.
What a dazzling transformation, from ship-rats
To astronauts, eclipsing
The first Argonauts to form a starry
Axle about which our Revolution spins.
If we're now lost at night or all at sea,
Look heavenwards, citizens, and be guided by
The bright Swiss galley in the sky.

'His Tongue's Red-hot Iron'

'His tongue's red-hot iron while
His charred veins stream with bile.'

For twelve years now I've secreted
Honeyed words in studious secret.

One day you'll see what's in them
Isn't festering venom

But an abundant sweetness.
Unlike hot Archilochus,

Crossed in love, whose barbed verse flayed
A father's pride and repaid

His lies, I'm not knotting
A rough noose for daddy's rotten

Neck. My anger's not personal.
It cries for country, for all

Laws scorned, and has peace on its lips
Even as it harries and nips.

So I arm with steel and fire
Against creatures of the mire.

Let no noxious vermin live
If humankind's to thrive.

Fille du vieux pasteur[3]

Fille du vieux pasteur, qui d'une main agile
Le soir emplis de lait trente vases d'argile,
Crains la génisse pourpre, au farouche regard,
Qui marche toujours seule et qui paît à l'écart.
Libre, elle lutte et fuit, intraitable et rebelle;
Tu ne presseras point sa féconde mamelle
A moins qu'avec adresse un de ses pieds lié
Sous un cuir souple et lent ne demeure plié.

Vu et fait à Catillon, près Forges, le 4 août 1792, et écrit à Gournay le
lendemain.

Sur la mort d'un enfant[4]

L'innocente victime, au terrestre séjour,
N'a vu que le printemps qui lui donna le jour.
Rien n'est resté de lui qu'un nom, un vain nuage,
Un souvenir, un songe, une invisible image.
Adieu, fragile enfant, échappé de nos bras;
Adieu, dans la maison d'où l'on ne revient pas.
Nous ne te verrons plus, quand de moissons couverte
La campagne d'été rend la ville déserte,
Dans l'enclos paternel nous ne te verrons plus,
De tes pieds, de tes mains, de tes flancs demi-nus,
Presser l'herbe et les fleurs dont les Nymphes de Seine
Couronnent tous les ans les coteaux de Lucienne.
L'axe de l'humble char à tes jeux destiné,
Par de fidèles mains avec toi promené,
Ne sillonnera plus les prés et le rivage.
Tes regards, ton murmure, obscur et doux langage,
N'inquiéteront plus nos soins officieux;
Nous ne recevrons plus, avec des cris joyeux,
Les efforts impuissants de ta bouche vermeille
A bégayer les sons offerts à ton oreille.
Adieu, dans la demeure où nous nous suivrons tous,
Où ta mère déjà tourne ses yeux jaloux.

A Shepherd's Girl

A shepherd's girl, you who, this warm evening,
Deftly fill thirty jars of clay with milk,
Beware of the crimson-coloured heifer
Which grazes on her own and walks apart.
Her eye is wild and she'll buck and run
Before you can raise a hand to her soft teats.
To milk her will need cunning, a supple
Tether nimbly stringing her fore leg back.

Witnessed at Catillon, near Forges-les-Eaux (Normandy), 4 August 1792, written at Gournay the following day.

On the Death of a Child

She only saw the spring that saw her birth.
Nothing remains of her brief time on earth
But a name that cleaves weakly to a dream
Recalled, a cloud whose contours blur and dim.
She slips from our arms, taking one last fond
Farewell into rooms receding into rooms beyond.
The harvest will empty the towns again,
Again meadow flowers along the Seine
Will constellate its rolling hills — but you
Will never be there now, never feel anew
Grass between small fingers and toes or soft skin
Bared to a sun — never to warm you again.
The little cart your father made you stands
Neglected. No more now will loving hands
Truckle you through meadows by the river.
To think we'll not hear your voice again, never
Solicitously lean to your limpid eyes
Nor jump up once more in joy and surprise
At that sound your red-red mouth half-formed, jabbering
In eager echo of our chattering.
Goodbye then — a year since they laid you low.
I watch your mother caught in the undertow.

Mai de moins de roses[5]

Mai de moins de roses, l'automne
De moins de pampres se couronne,
Moins d'épis flottent en moissons,
Que sur mes lèvres, sur ma lyre,
Fanny, tes regards, ton sourire,
Ne font éclore de chansons.

Les secrets pensers de mon âme
Sortent en paroles de flamme,
A ton nom doucement émus.
Ainsi la nacre industrieuse
Jette sa perle précieuse,
Honneur des sultanes d'Ormuz.

Ainsi, sur son mûrier fertile,
Le ver de Cathay mêle et file
Sa trame étincelante d'or.
Viens: mes Muses, pour ta parure,
De leur soie immortelle et pure
Versent un plus riche trésor.

Les perles de la poésie
Forment, sous leurs doigts d'ambroisie,
D'un collier le brillant contour.
Viens, Fanny: que ma main suspende
Sur ton sein cette noble offrande.

May Sees Fewer Roses Flower

May sees fewer roses flower,
Autumn sheaves and vines look duller,
Eclipsed in brilliance and in number
By songs, Fanny, my glad heart sings,
By the many lovely songs
Blooming in your eyes like summer.

And like those specks of grit or sand
That swell to lustrous pearls around
The tawny necks of Persian queens,
The tiny note of your name sounded
Stirs in me such music round it
I become a symphony of strings.

The wondrous silkworms of China
Spin patterns in the air finer
Than a goldsmith's subtle tracing;
Finer still, silk of my verse
Will weave for you a lyric dress
With love for cloth and sighs for lacing.

So buds and pearls and silk become
So many metaphors of song,
Of love lightly lain about
Your beautiful white shoulders.
Come my love, let love enfold us.

Fanny, l'heureux mortel qui près de toi respire[6]

Fanny, l'heureux mortel qui près de toi respire
Sait, à te voir parler et rougir et sourire,
De quels hôtes divins le ciel est habité.
La grâce, la candeur, la naïve innocence
  Ont, depuis ton enfance,
De tout ce qui peut plaire enrichi ta beauté.

Sur tes traits, ou ton âme imprime sa noblesse,
Elles ont su mêler aux roses de jeunesse
Ces roses de pudeur, charmes plus séduisants;
Et remplir tes regards, tes lèvres, ton langage,
  De ce miel dont le sage
Cherche lui-même en vain à défendre ses sens.

Oh! que n'ai-je moi seul tout l'éclat et la gloire
Que donnent les talents, la beauté, la victoire,
Pour fixer sur moi seul ta pensée et tes yeux!
Que, loin de moi, ton cœur fût plein de ma présence,
  Comme, dans ton absence,
Ton aspect bien-aimé m'est présent en tous lieux!

Je pense: Elle était là. Tous disaient: 'Qu'elle est belle!'
Tels furent ses regards, sa démarche fut telle,
Et tels ses vêtements, sa voix et ses discours.
Sur ce gazon assise, et dominant la plaine,
  Des méandres de Seine,
Rêveuse, elle suivait les obliques détours.

Ainsi dans les forêts j'erre avec ton image:
Ainsi le jeune faon, dans son désert sauvage,
D'un plomb volant percé, précipite ses pas.
Il emporte en fuyant sa mortelle blessure;
  Couché près d'une eau pure,
Palpitant, hors d'haleine, il attend le trépas.

Fanny, It's Some Lucky Guy

Fanny it's some lucky guy
Who gets to breathe the air you breathe
And for all your smiles and blushes
Your dress don't hide your angel wings
I bet you were the cutest girl
With no notion of your grace

And now you glow like a summer rose
Though you sway just out of reach
And there's something proud in your swaying head
Red petals like full lips
It would take a hard hard heart
Not to bend to you and breathe

So just for once let me be the one
You pick out in the room
Though I'm not exactly what they call a catch
Let your eyes see me as mine see you
Every silhouette my profile
Every sky your shade of blue

I come when you're gone to hear others say
Just how beautiful you are
Your eyes are gemstones your walk a poem
Just divine what you said and wore
You sat on the lawn and let your thoughts roll
With the twisting river below

I walk in the woods with a picture of you
Which means I walk alone
Just me and this bullet lodged in my side
That you shot off without even knowing
So I'll stumble on to a stream and some shade
A restful corner to die in.

A Marie-Anne-Charlotte Corday[7]

Quoi! tandis que partout, ou sincères ou feintes,
Des lâches, des pervers, les larmes et les plaintes
Consacrent leur Marat parmi les immortels;
Et que, prêtre orgueilleux de cette idole vile,
Des fanges du Parnasse un impudent reptile
Vomit un hymne infâme au pied de ses autels;

La Vérité se tait! Dans sa bouche glacée,
Des liens de la peur sa langue embarrassée
Dérobe un juste hommage aux exploits glorieux!
Vivre est-il donc si doux? De quel prix est la vie,
Quand, sous un joug honteux la pensée asservie,
Tremblante, au fond du cœur se cache à tous les yeux?

Non, non, je ne veux point t'honorer en silence,
Toi qui crus par ta mort ressusciter la France,
Et dévouas tes jours à punir des forfaits.
Le glaive arma ton bras, fille grande et sublime,
Pour faire honte aux Dieux, pour réparer leur crime,
Quand d'un homme à ce monstre ils donnèrent les traits.

Le noir serpent, sorti de sa caverne impure,
A donc vu rompre enfin sous ta main ferme et sûre
Le venimeux tissu de ses jours abhorrés!
Aux entrailles du tigre, à ses dents homicides,
Tu vins redemander et les membres livides,
Et le sang des humains qu'il avait dévorés!

Son œil mourant t'a vue, en ta superbe joie,
Féliciter ton bras, et contempler ta proie.
Ton regard lui disait: 'Va, tyran furieux,
Va, cours frayer la route aux tyrans tes complices.
Te baigner dans le sang fut tes seules délices;
Baigne-toi dans le tien, et reconnais des Dieux.'

La Grèce, ô fille illustre, admirant ton courage,
Épuiserait Paros, pour placer ton image
Auprès d'Harmodius, auprès de son ami;
Et des chœurs sur ta tombe, en une sainte ivresse,
Chanteraient Némésis, la tardive Déesse,
Qui frappe le méchant sur son trône endormi.

To Marie-Anne-Charlotte Corday

What! while all around, with sincere or feigned
Tears and moans, the cowardly and perverse
Enshrine their Marat among the immortals;
While the proud priest of this loathsome idol,
A reptile slunk from the filth of Parnassus, spews
An insolent hymn over its altars,

Truth is struck dumb! Its mouth moves coldly,
Gagged on fear, its tongue too thick to offer up
Praise rightfully due to glorious deeds!
Is it so sweet to live? What is life worth
When thought, enslaved under a shameful yoke,
Cowers in the heart's well, hidden from all eyes?

No, no, I will not honour you in silence,
Who hoped your death might regenerate France,
Who devoted your days to avenging wrongs,
Magnificent girl, who took up the sword
To shame the gods and atone for their crime
When they gave this monster the traits of a man.

From his soiled cavern this black snake slithered
To see the venomous tissue of its abhorrent life
Severed at last by your firm and steady hand!
From this tiger's maw and its murderous teeth
You made a reckoning with the man-eater
For all the blood drunk, the white limbs gorged on.

His dimming sight beheld you, exultant,
Thank the gods for your strength, contemplating
Your work. Your eyes spoke: 'Go, rabid tyrant,
Go pave the way for your fellow mad dogs.
Bathing in blood was your only delight:
Bathe in your own as divine justice commands.'

Illustrious girl, Greece in admiration
Of your courage would mine Paros of all marble
To statue you among its tyrant-slayers;
And choirs at your graveside in holy trance
Would sing of late-avenging Nemesis
Smiting the smiling criminal enthroned.

Mais la France à la hache abandonne ta tête.
C'est au monstre égorgé qu'on prépare une fête,
Parmi ses compagnons, tous dignes de son sort.
Oh! quel noble dédain fit sourire ta bouche,
Quand un brigand, vengeur de ce brigand farouche,
Crut te faire pâlir aux menaces de mort!

C'est lui qui dut pâlir; et tes juges sinistres,
Et notre affreux sénat, et ses affreux ministres,
Quand, à leur tribunal, sans crainte et sans appui,
Ta douceur, ton langage et simple et magnanime,
Leur apprit qu'en effet, tout puissant qu'est le crime,
Qui renonce à la vie est plus puissant que lui.

Longtemps, sous les dehors d'une allégresse aimable,
Dans ses détours profonds ton âme impénétrable
Avait tenu cachés les destins du pervers.
Ainsi, dans le secret amassant la tempête,
Rit un beau ciel d'azur, qui cependant s'apprête
A foudroyer les monts, et soulever les mers.

Belle, jeune, brillante, aux bourreaux amenée,
Tu semblais t'avancer sur le char d'hyménée,
Ton front resta paisible, et ton regard serein.
Calme sur l'échafaud, tu méprisas la rage
D'un peuple abject, servile et fécond en outrage,
Et qui se croit alors et libre et souverain.

La vertu seule est libre. Honneur de notre histoire,
Notre immortel opprobre y vit avec ta gloire.
Seule tu fus un homme, et vengeas les humains.
Et nous, eunuques vils, troupeau lâche et sans âme,
Nous savons répéter quelques plaintes de femme,
Mais le fer pèserait à nos débiles mains.

Non; tu ne pensais pas qu'aux mânes de la France
Un seul traître immolé suffît à sa vengeance,
Ou tirât du chaos ses débris dispersés.
Tu voulais, enflammant les courages timides,
Réveiller les poignards sur tous ces parricides,
De rapine, de sang, d'infamie engraissés.

Un scélérat de moins rampe dans cette fange.
La Vertu t'applaudit. De sa mâle louange
Entends, belle héroïne, entends l'auguste voix.
O Vertu, le poignard, seul espoir de la terre,
Est ton arme sacrée, alors que le tonnerre
Laisse régner le crime, et te vend à ses lois.

Instead France offers up your head to the axe
While festivals for the monster you killed
Are planned by those fit to meet the same fate.
Oh, what noble scorn set a smile on your lips
When one lout, to avenge his more loutish idol,
Thought he could make you blanch with threats of death!

He was to turn pale as did your grim judges,
As did our feared senate, its feared mouthpieces:
Before their court, fearless and unfriended,
Your calmness, your simple, noble language
Affirmed that, almighty though crime may seem,
One embracing death is mightier still.

For a long time then your amiable air
Hid in the depths of an inscrutable soul
The fate awaiting your debased enemy.
Likewise in secret the clearest blue sky
Foments the coming storm, gathering itself
To blast the mountain peaks and upheave the seas.

Beautiful shining youth, led to slaughter
As though a bride riding superbly to church,
Your brow untroubled and your gaze serene.
Calm on the scaffold you scorned the fury
Of an abject, servile mob, foaming with insult,
Declaring itself still sovereign and free.

Only virtue is free. Our undying shame
Abides with your glory, your historic feat.
You alone were man enough to save mankind
While we, soulless, craven crowd, vilely unmanned,
We know how to wail and moan like women —
But the knife? Too weighty for our feeble hands.

No. You did not think that all the shades of France
Could be avenged by one lone traitor's death
Or its scattered debris salvaged from chaos.
You sought to fire the timid with courage,
To unsheathe blades to puncture these parricides
Bloated on infamy, rapine and blood.

One villain less now crawls amid this filth.
The virtuous applaud you. Lovely hero,
Hear their solemn tributes, their manly praise.
Ah, virtue, when the gods avert their gaze,
And let criminals rule and pawn you to their laws,
Bless the dagger drawn as your last hope on earth.

Fragment: Épilogue d'*Hermès*[8]

O mon fils, mon Hermès, ma plus belle espérance,
O fruit des longs travaux de ma persévérance,
Toi, l'objet le plus cher des veilles de dix ans,
Qui m'as coûté des soins et si doux et si lents;
Confident de ma joie et remède à mes peines;
Sur les lointaines mers, sur les terres lointaines,
Compagnon bien-aimé de mes pas incertains,
O mon fils, aujourd'hui quels seront tes destins?
Une mère longtemps se cache ses alarmes.
Elle-même à son fils veut attacher ses armes;
Mais quand il faut partir, ses bras, ses faibles bras
Ne peuvent sans terreur l'envoyer aux combats.
Dans la France pour toi que faut-il que j'espère?
Jadis, enfant chéri, dans la maison d'un père
Qui te regardait naître et grandir sous ses yeux,
Tu pouvais, sans péril, disciple curieux,
Sur tout ce qui frappait ton enfance attentive
Donner un libre essor à ta langue naïve.
Plus de père aujourd'hui! Le mensonge est puissant;
Il règne. Dans ses mains luit un fer menaçant.
De la vérité sainte il déteste l'approche.
Il craint que son regard ne lui fasse un reproche;
Que ses traits, sa candeur, sa voix, son souvenir,
Tout mensonge qu'il est, ne le fassent pâlir.
Mais la vérité seule est une, est éternelle.
Le mensonge varie; et l'homme, trop fidèle,
Change avec lui. Pour lui les humains sont constants
Et roulent de mensonge en mensonge flottants.
...
Perdu, n'existant plus qu'en un docte cerveau,
Le français ne sera dans ce monde nouveau
Qu'une écriture antique et non plus un langage.
O, si tu vis encore, alors peut-être un sage,
Près d'une lampe assis, dans l'étude plongé,
Te retrouvant poudreux, obscur, demi rongé,
Voudra creuser le sens de tes lignes pensantes.
Il verra si du moins tes feuilles innocentes
Méritaient ces rumeurs, ces tempêtes, ces cris,
Qui vont sur toi sans doute éclater dans Paris.

Fragment: Epilogue of 'Hermes'

I had a poem I loved like a son,
Bodying forth my best hopes and dreams, one
Cherished and fashioned over ten long years,
A solace in grief, in joy a boon. There was
Not one day without him as companion
In travels abroad over land and sea, not one
Step taken without him. A treasured presence,
A dear son whose fate now hangs in the balance.

For a long time mothers might fret in silence.
They might fire their son to a bold defence
Of hearth and homeland, but when the call-up comes
Their thin arms tighten round his neck and low moans
Wrack them.
                            What should I hope for you, my son,
In France today? Before, in the loving home
Your father made for you, lit by his kind gaze,
You would feed your curiosity, days
Filled with letting your ingenuous tongue run
On any thing that caught your eye or ear. Gone
Now — both loving home and father! Only
Lies are left. Liars alone prevail. They
Rule unchallenged or finger the blade each time
A righteous voice ventures to unmask them.
It's true, when some brave soul speaks up, they blench
A moment, look shifty and retire. At length,
However, they know, we know, that the harsh
Unblinking glare of truth always proves too much
For us. Like lies we're prolific, versatile,
Inconstant, shifting, perfectly disloyal.

And in this brave new world what shall French become?
Not a language any more — a hieroglyph, a rune
Lost to all but a dusty scholar's musings.
A squinting scribe, hunched among his few things,
Might then pore over you, my poem, my son,
Tracing your worm-shot, obscure lines in the wan
Light of his lamps, scanning for your occult sense.
He'll surmise at least if your innocence
Warranted the vicious din all Paris has —
Or doubtless will — set shrieking at your ears.

Fragment: Un vulgaire assassin va chercher les ténèbres[9]

Un vulgaire [assassin] va chercher les ténèbres;
    Il nie, il jure sur l'autel.
Mais nous, grands, libres, fiers, à nos exploits fun[èbres],
    A nos [turpitudes] célèbres,
Nous voulons attacher un éclat imm[ortel].

De l'oubli tacit[urne] et de son onde n[oire]
    Nous savons détour[ner] le cours.
Nous appelons sur nous l'étern[elle] mém[oire].
    Nos [forfaits], notre unique his[toire],
Parent de nos cités les brillants carrefours.

O [gardes] de L[ouis] sous les voûtes royales
    Par nos [ménades] déchirés,
Vos têtes sur un fer ont pour nos Bacch[anales]
    Orné nos portes [triomph]ales.
A ces bronzes hideux, nos [monuments] sacrés,

Tout ce [peuple] hébété que nul rem[ords] ne touche,
    Cruel même dans son [repos],
Vient sourire aux succès de sa r[age] [farouche]
    Et, la soif encore à la bouche,
Ruminer tout l[e sang] dont il a bu les flots.

Arts dignes de nos yeux! pompe et magnif[icence]
    Digne de notre [liberté],
Digne des vils [tyrans] qui dév[astent] la Fr[ance],
    Digne de l'atroce démence
Du stupide D[avid] qu'autrefois j'ai chanté.

Your Common Murderer Goes to Ground

Your common murderer goes to ground,
Swears blind it wasn't him.
Not us, though, the Great, the Free, the Proud
Whose dismal public vices stand
As our most glorious claim to fame.

Even when rightful obscurity knocks,
We just slip out the back door,
Back into the limelight and the history books
Where our crimes light up like fireworks
Our garish triumphs in city squares.

Royal guardsmen had their heads hacked off
Under antique porticos
By wild party-girls now come to laugh
At their livid trophies stuck on staffs
In lieu of more tasteful statues.

Not that this dazed rabble would flinch
From further acts of lazy cruelty.
How they paint the town red! but binge
On blood not wine. It dribbles down their chins
From smiles cracked recalling some brutality.

Street art worthy of our gaze, gold-plate and chintz
Fit to adorn our freedoms,
Fit for the tin-pot tyrants who ravage France,
Fit too for the power-crazed rants
Of stupid David whose praise I once sung.

A Byzance[10]

Byzance, mon berceau, jamais tes janissaires
Du musulman paisible ont-ils forcé le seuil?
Vont-ils jusqu'en son lit, nocturnes émissaires,
  Porter l'épouvante et le deuil?

Son harem ne connaît, invisible retraite,
Le choix, ni les projets, ni le nom des vizirs.
Là, sûr du lendemain, il repose sa tête,
  Sans craindre, au sein de ses plaisirs,

Que cent nouvelles lois qu'une nuit a fait naître,
De juges assassins un tribunal pervers,
Lancent sur son réveil, avec le nom de traître,
  La mort, la ruine, ou les fers.

Tes mœurs et ton Coran sur ton sultan farouche
Veillent, le glaive nu, s'il croyait tout pouvoir;
S'il osait tout braver, et dérober sa bouche
  Au frein de l'antique devoir.

Voilà donc une digue où la toute-puissance
Voit briser le torrent de ses vastes progrès.
Liberté qui nous fuis, tu ne fuis point Byzance;
  Tu planes sur ses minarets.

To Constantinople

Constantinople, city I was born in,
Do your royal guards force the peaceful Turk's door?
Or, his bed at night defiled, litter his floor
With the bloodied sheets of a house in mourning?

His harem remains a hidden retreat.
Ignorant of the plans of faceless vizirs,
There his head rests in the soft lap of pleasures,
Safe from harm and free from the threat

Of being dragged, half-awake, to a room where
A snarling, perverse court sits in judgement,
Whose curled lips drip ruin, death, imprisonment,
As daily new treasons are plucked from the air.

Your Quran, your customs, cool as steel,
Trim any ambition a fierce sultan might nurse
To spurn the old ways, defy laws — or worse,
Scorn duty with irreligious zeal.

Here, then, stands a bulwark that arrests
The swelling torrent of his unchecked powers.
The freedom that flees *us* still soars over your towers,
Constantinople, your slim minarets.

A Versailles[11]

O Versaille, ô bois, ô portiques,
Marbres vivants, berceaux antiques,
Par les Dieux et les rois Élysée embelli,
A ton aspect, dans ma pensée,
Comme sur l'herbe aride une fraîche rosée,
Coule un peu de calme et d'oubli.

Paris me semble un autre empire,
Dès que chez toi je vois sourire
Mes pénates secrets couronnés de rameaux;
D'où souvent les monts et les plaines
Vont dirigeant mes pas aux campagnes prochaines,
Sous de triples cintres d'ormeaux.

Les chars, les royales merveilles,
Des gardes les nocturnes veilles,
Tout a fui; des grandeurs tu n'es plus le séjour:
Mais le sommeil, la solitude,
Dieux jadis inconnus, et les arts, et l'étude
Composent aujourd'hui ta cour.

Ah! malheureux! à ma jeunesse
Une oisive et morne paresse
Ne laisse plus goûter les studieux loisirs.
Mon âme, d'ennui consumée,
S'endort dans les langueurs. Louange et renommée
N'inquiètent plus mes désirs.

L'abandon, l'obscurité, l'ombre,
Une paix taciturne et sombre,
Voilà tous mes souhaits. Cache mes tristes jours,
Et nourris, s'il faut que je vive,
De mon pâle flambeau la clarté fugitive,
Aux douces chimères d'amours.

L'âme n'est point encor flétrie,
La vie encor n'est point tarie,
Quand un regard nous trouble et le cœur et la voix.
Qui cherche les pas d'une belle,
Qui peut ou s'égayer ou gémir auprès d'elle,
De ses jours peut porter le poids.

To Versailles

I've never been so moved by the old place.
I'd call it an Elysium, I mean,
If that's not too grand, a palace
Though, and such a glorious one

With ancient gods in mottled marble —
Festooned carriages once ploughed its gravel
Magicked up by the click of royal
Fingers. The guards at night must have seen

Some stuff on their rounds, off paths
Through the bushes... And now look at it:
Sleepy, deserted, solemn, dead
Perfect for me though to stroll through,

A balm, I'd say, for my mind and body,
Like the dew that settles on desire paths,
Those shortcuts through the grass
Worn yellow and parched by too much footfall.

It's a million miles from Paris,
That's for certain. I love its
Leafy alleyways, the elm trees holding hands
Over my head like that dance

Where couples fold into a tunnel of love.
From here you can see the countryside.
From here you can see my childhood,
Or at least my youth, now jaded

And out of sorts with fame and fortune.
So again, the perfect place to lose oneself.
All the grandeur and gloom, the faded
Glories, the shabby genteel trees

In autumn casting shadows
Through which we walked once to the riverbank
And where an unspoken love still haunts
The path and I know suddenly

The exact spot where I didn't say
What I should have. So now
I mouth her name to the rustling trees
And spy on our ghosts conversing,

J'aime; je vis. Heureux rivage!
Tu conserves sa noble image,
Son nom, qu'à tes forêts j'ose apprendre le soir;
Quand, l'âme doucement émue,
J'y reviens méditer l'instant où je l'ai vue,
Et l'instant où je dois la voir.

Pour elle seule encore abonde
Cette source, jadis féconde,
Qui coulait de ma bouche en sons harmonieux.
Sur mes lèvres tes bosquets sombres
Forment pour elle encor ces poétiques nombres,
Langage d'amour et des Dieux.

Ah! témoin des succès du crime,
Si l'homme juste et magnanime
Pouvait ouvrir son cœur à la félicité,
Versailles, tes routes fleuries,
Ton silence, fertile en belles rêveries,
N'auraient que joie et volupté.

Mais souvent tes vallons tranquilles,
Tes sommets verts, tes frais asiles,
Tout à coup à mes yeux s'enveloppent de deuil.
J'y vois errer l'ombre livide
D'un peuple d'innocents, qu'un tribunal perfide
Précipite dans le cercueil.

My breath, my flesh, heavy and intrusive.
And there the words come. Tumbling like a brook,
The words stream through the dusky copses,
Diffracted by branch and trunk

To make a strange evening harmony.
This light would be yet more sensual,
The stillness more resonant, if it weren't
For knowing the hot proximity of crime.

A wrong turn brings me face to face with wraiths,
Once people, carted to a courtroom,
Then more carts taking cadavers off,
Their sepulchre a plain communal pit.

Voûtes du Panthéon[12]

Voûtes du Panthéon, quel mort illustre et rare
    S'ouvre vos dômes glorieux?
Pourquoi vois-je David qui larmoie, et prépare
    Sa palette qui fait des Dieux?
O ciel! faut-il le croire! ô destins! ô fortune!
    O cercueil arrosé de pleurs!
Oh! que ne puis-je ouïr Barère à la tribune,
    Gros de pathos et de douleurs!
Quelle nouvelle en France et quel canon d'alarmes
    Dans tous les cœurs a retenti!
Les fils des Jacobins leur *adressent* des larmes.
    Brissot, qui n'a jamais menti,
Dit avoir vu dans l'air d'exhalaisons impures
    Un noir nuage tournoyer,
Du sang, et de la fange, et toutes les ordures
    Dont se forme un épais bourbier;
Et soutient que c'était la sale et vilaine âme
    Par qui Marat avait vécu.
De ses jours florissants, par la main d'une femme,
    Ce lien aimable est rompu!
Le Calvados en rit. Mais la potence pleure.
    Déjà par un fer meurtrier
Pelletier fut placé dans l'auguste demeure.
    Marat vaut mieux que Pelletier.
Nul n'aima tant le sang, n'eut tant de soif des crimes.
    Qu'on parle d'un vil scélérat,
Bien que Lacroix, Bourdon, soient des mortels sublimes,
    Nous ne pensons tous qu'à Marat.
Il était né de droit vassal de la potence.
    Il était son plus cher trésor.
Console-toi, gibet. Tu sauveras la France.
    Pour tes bras la Montagne encor
Nourrit bien des héros dans ses nobles repaires:
    Le Gendre, *élève de Caton*,
Le grand Collot d'Herbois, fier *patron* des galères,
    Plus d'un Robespierre, et Danton,
Thuriot, et Chabot; enfin toute la bande;
    Et club, commune, tribunal;
Mais qui peut les compter? Je te les recommande.
    Tu feras l'appel nominal.
Pour chanter à ces saints de dignes litanies,
    L'un demande Anacharsis Clotz;

Vaults of the Pantheon

Vaults of the Pantheon, what illustrious man among men
Is welcomed in your hallowed halls?
Why does David wipe a tear? Whom does he now ready
To immortalize in oils?
O Gods! Can it be true? Truly, the worst of days!
A simple coffin dark with tears!
Oh to hear Barère at the bar fulsome in
Pathetic eulogies!
The news ripples through the crowd, the cannons sound,
Confirming deepest fears!
The Jacobins *dispatch* sincerest sympathies
While Brissot, the unimpeachable,
Declares he saw the air grow rank and black
With a fetid stain that whirled
Flies and filth and all the stinking trash that forms
A seething cesspool,
Claiming it was nothing but the purest mark
Of Marat's foul departing soul.
To think it was a woman's hand that cut him down
In the full flower of his fame.
The rebel West might cheer — but not the guillotine.
Lepeletier before him:
Knifed, laid out, mourned and moved to the Pantheon.
But the stakes were not the same.
In the potlatch of heads on pikes Marat ruled supreme.
Lacroix or Bourdon, say,
Could rouse the mob but only the 'people's friend'
Could set them on to slaughter.
In turn the guillotine would love him too
Who fed it like no other.
Yet, hangman, take heart. Marat might be gone
But the Jacobins still teem
With heroes who aspire to nobler crimes:
Legendre whose measured screams
Second Collot setting free his galley-slaves,
Or Danton, Robespierre,
Chabot, Thuriot, and many of their kind,
Bent placeman, judge or mayor —
Too many here to count. But *so* much to admire.
Let the hangman call them out.
Though who among these genii might best bleat
Or bellow thanks for Marat?

L'autre veut Cabanis, ou d'autres grands génies;
    Et qui Grouvelle, et qui Laclos.
Mais non; nous entendrons ces oraisons funèbres
    De la bouche du bon Garat;
Puis tu les enverras tous au fond des ténèbres
    Lécher le cul du bon Marat.
Que la tombe sur vous, sur vos reliques chères,
    Soit légère, ô mortels sacrés;
Pour qu'avec moins d'effort, par les dogues vos frères,
    Vos cadavres soient déchirés.

Par le citoyen Archiloque Mastigophore

Anacharsis, Cabanis, Grouvelle, Laclos?
None will do. Instead, let Garat
Intone a homespun dirge and let others
Snivelling behind the hearse
Be packed inside so they can better lick
Their idol's poxy arse.
And may the earth lie lightly on your bones,
Dear Marat! Hallowed friends!
So pitbull and mastiff, your drooling brothers,
Can briskly dig them up again.

By citizen Archilochus Mastigophorus.

O mon esprit, au sein des cieux[13]

Strophe I
O mon esprit, au sein des cieux,
Loin de tes noirs chagrins, une ardente allégresse
    Te transporte au banquet des Dieux,
    Lorsque ta haine vengeresse,
Rallumée à l'aspect et du meurtre et du sang,
Ouvre de ton carquois l'inépuisable flanc.
De là vole aux méchants ta flèche redoutée,
    D'un fiel vertueux humectée,
Qu'au défaut de la foudre, esclave du plus fort,
    Sur tous ces pontifes du crime,
Par qui la France, aveugle et stupide victime,
Palpite et se débat contre une longue mort,
    Lance ta fureur magnanime.

Antistrophe I
    Tu crois, d'un éternel flambeau
Éclairant les forfaits d'une horde ennemie,
    Défendre à la nuit du tombeau
    D'ensevelir leur infamie.
Déjà tu penses voir, des bouts de l'univers,
Sur la foi de ma lyre, au nom de ces pervers,
Frémir l'horreur publique; et d'honneur et de gloire
    Fleurir ma tombe et ta mémoire;
Comme autrefois tes Grecs accouraient à des jeux,
    Quand l'amoureux fleuve d'Élide,
Eut de traîtres punis vu triompher Alcide;
Ou quand l'arc Pythien d'un reptile fangeux
    Eut purgé les champs de Phocide.

Epode I
    Vain espoir! inutile soin!
Ramper est des humains l'ambition commune;
    C'est leur plaisir; c'est leur besoin.
Voir, fatigue leurs yeux; juger les importune;
    Ils laissent juger la fortune,
Qui fait juste celui qu'elle fait tout-puissant:
Ce n'est point la vertu, c'est la seule victoire
    Qui donne et l'honneur et la gloire:
Teint du sang des vaincus, tout glaive est innocent.

There's Elation in My Pain

VOICE(S) 1: Stage right
There's elation in my pain, or it's more that
The spectacle of daily torture, murder and blood fills me with
A pale and oddly ethereal lightheadedness
A long way from pedestrian worry or everyday depression
And so my mind, unburdened, feels the invigorating possibility of
Indulging to the utmost my vengeful hatred, my bottomless contempt.
It borders on profligacy the way in which I unleash shaft
After shaft of steel-tipped scorn at
The presumptuous Mafiosi running France like a drugs cartel.
Don't get me wrong, I'm no Zeus hurling lightning bolts
(Now a logo for the state police), no, I'm more like
The old dog's owner who has the largesse of spirit
To put her down with a generous shot of bitter-tasting morphine.

VOICE(S) 2: Stage left
So you start to think that your vehement denunciations
Will be like a blazing eye sewn open emitting
A sempiternal stream of light on this pack of fraudsters
And crooks whom you detest so that they can never just skit
Like roaches under the skirting-boards of history.
And as you and I are one and the same,
As you vivisect them publicly and I sing about it,
We'll both have bouquets sprayed on our tomb
And crowds will hold a minute's deafening execration
Each year in our honour and to our enemies' everlasting shame.
It'll be like the ancient Greeks who
Flocked to cheer Heracles the mythic pest controller
Or Apollo when he studded a monstrous python with arrows.

VOICE(S) 3: Centre-stage
Fat chance of that! Don't fool yourself that people will do
Anything but crawl on their belly, kow-tow to the most powerful.
You know it — they get a kick out of getting kicked.
They can't be fagged with the hassle and faff of seeing
Things clearly, with making a call, let alone taking a stand.
Better leave that to fate, to chance, same thing really, because what is right
Is what you're told is right by your betters. The only glory
In this world falls to those who call the photo-op. The peace prize goes to
First to the top of a Himalaya of corpses.

Strophe II

Que tant d'opprimés expirants
Aillent aux cieux enfin réveiller le supplice;
Que sur ces monstres dévorants
Son bras d'airain s'appesantisse;
Qu'ils tombent: à l'instant vois-tu leurs noms flétris,
Par leur peuple vénal leurs cadavres meurtris,
Et pour jamais transmise à la publique ivresse
Ta louange avec leur bassesse?
Mais si Mars est pour eux, leurs vertus, leurs bienfaits,
Sont bénis de la terre entière.
Tout s'obscurcit auprès de la splendeur guerrière;
Elle éblouit les yeux, et sur les noirs forfaits
Étend un voile de lumière.

Antistrophe II

Dès lors l'étranger étonné
Se tait avec respect devant leur sceptre immense;
Leur peuple à leurs pieds enchaîné,
Vantant jusques à leur clémence,
Nous voue à la risée, à l'opprobre, aux tourments,
Nous, de la vertu libre indomptables amants.
Humains, lâche troupeau!... Mais qu'importent au sage
Votre blâme, votre suffrage,
Vos encens, vos poignards, et de flux en reflux
Vos passions précipitées?
Il nous faut tous mourir. A sa vie ajoutées,
Au prix du déshonneur, quelques heures de plus
Lui sembleraient trop achetées.

Epode II

Lui, grands Dieux! courtisan menteur,
De sa raison céleste abandonner le faîte,
Pour descendre à votre hauteur!
En lui-même affermi, comme l'antique athlète
Sur le sol, où son pied s'arrête,
Il reste, inébranlable à tout effort mortel;
Et laisse avec dédain ce vulgaire imbécile,
Toujours turbulent et servile,
Flotter de maître en maître et d'autel en autel.

VOICE(s) I: Stage right
So many dead calling for justice, so many souls
Aching for their butchers to be in turn brought low —
That they be crushed, that they be annihilated now and forever.
But *actually* do you see their names shrivelling
On lips or a mercenary people stamping on the bodies
Of their overlords like peasants dancing in a wine-press?
Is your name praised to the skies
While your enemies are publicly reviled in endless, heady jubilation?
Is it not the case that whoever has the guns has the glory?
Light glancing off epaulettes, helmets and light
Weaponry is not without aesthetic effect.
The vapour trails hatched by their whooshing jets demarcate
A dazing white no-fly zone over the truth.

VOICE(s): Stage left
From this point on, foreign powers fall silent before
The awful, juddering state machine. They see a people ground beneath
A heel taken off their necks just long enough for them to thank
Their oppressors for their kindness and clemency, indeed most grateful
For this brief opportunity to mock and scorn us, and wish us
Death by a thousand cuts, we the unyielding guerrillas of love, liberty and
                                                    the common good.
What a cowardly herd, what a farm of craven slaves! Your fraternal embrace —
There, just a bit more, there, to plant the knife
Between the shoulder blades — your praise and blame
Are like a bottle passed between drunkards sloshing from
Hand to hand, from one extreme passion to another, that means
Strictly nothing to the smartest, the most dispassionate amongst us.
We're all born to die. Let's not cheapen life with a shabby exit.

VOICE(s): Centre-stage
For Christ's sake! Really, do you think that he or she who's smart enough
To see your little game would stoop to concur with your people!
Look to our sporting legends to understand, see how
The true athlete holds herself, remains unmoved
And unmoveable while all around her — you, in fact —
Swirl like tickertape, to a faltering chorus of cheers and boos,
Detritus blown about her feet, and in its midst
The only indication of her shared mortality is
A wry, contemptuous tic at the corner of her lips saying nothing.

On dit que le dédain froid et silencieux[14]

On dit que le dédain froid et silencieux
  Devint une ardente colère,
Lorsque le *Moniteur* vous eut mis sous les yeux
  Le sot fatras du sot Barère;
Qu'au phœbus convulsif de l'ignare pédant,
  De honte et de terreur troublées,
Votre front se souvint de ce Thrace impudent,
  Qui vous eût toutes violées.
On dit plus: mais je sais combien chez nos plaisants
  Grâce, pucelage, et faconde,
Exposent une belle à des bruits médisants:
  Ils veulent que sur cet immonde
Vous ayez, mais tout bas, aux effroyables sons
  D'apostrophes trop masculines,
Joint pied-plat, gredin, cuistre, et d'autres maudissons,
  Peu faits pour vos lèvres divines;
Dignes de lui, d'accord; mais indignes de vous.
  Ces gens n'ont point votre langage;
N'apprenez point le leur. Un ignoble courroux
  Justifie un ignoble outrage.

I'm Told You've Never Been So Angry

I'm told you've never been so angry,
Shocked out of your cold contempt
By the mindless drivel a daily rag
Reported from our parliament.
This ignoramus misquoting Latin,
This tin-eared, barking lawyer
Outraged you like the hand up the skirt
Tried on by a junior minister.
Sure, I know they attack you, hate that you're svelte,
Quick-witted and pretty,
Not to mention, effortlessly out of their league.
But this time, others tell me,
You couldn't help it: along with choice putdowns
That would make a navvy blush,
You treated this worm to swindler, oaf, and cretin,
(Albeit under your sweet breath)
Which, I admit, is spot on, but also
Beneath you. These people trade
In filth. Don't let an ugly anger smear you
With the dirt they hurl with pride.

Vingt barques, faux tissus de planches fugitives[15]

Vingt barques, faux tissus de planches fugitives,
 S'entr'ouvrant au milieu des eaux,
Ont-elles par milliers dans les gouffres de Loire
 Vomi des captifs enchaînés,
Au proconsul Carrier, implacable après boire,
 Pour son passe-temps amenés?
Et ces porte-plumets, ces commis de carnage,
 Ces noirs accusateurs Fouquiers,
Ces Dumas, ces jurés, horrible aréopage
 De voleurs et de meurtriers,
Les ai-je poursuivis jusqu'en leurs bacchanales,
 Lorsque, les yeux encore ardents,
Attablés, le bordeaux de chaleurs plus brutales
 Allumant leurs fronts impudents,
Ivres et bégayant la crapule et les crimes,
 Ils rappellent avec des ris
Leurs meurtres d'auj[ourd'hui], leurs futures victimes;
 Et parmi les chansons, les cris,
Trouvent deçà delà, sous leur main, sous leur bo[uche],
 De femmes un vénal essaim,
Dépouilles du vaincu, transfuges de sa couche
 Pour la couche de l'assassin.
Car ce sexe ébloui de tout semblant de gloire,
 Né l'héritage du plus fort,
Quel que soit le vainqueur, suit toujours la victoire;
 D'une lèvre arbitre de mort
Étale le baiser, le brigue avec audace;
 Et pour nulle oppressive main
Leur jupe n'est pesante et l'épingle tenace
 N'a de pointe autour de leur sein.
Le remords est, dit-on, l'enfer où tout s'expie.
 Quel remords agite le flanc,
Tourmente le sommeil du [tribunal] impie
 Qui mange, boit, rote du sang?
Car qui peut noblement de leur bande perverse
 Rendre les attentats fameux?
Ces monstres sont impurs; la lance qui les perce
 Sort impure, infecte comme eux.

Twenty False-bottomed Boats

Twenty false-bottomed boats cracked
Open in the choppy
Icy waters of the Loire spewed
Their chained human
Cargo by the writhing thousands
One long awful moan
A plumed hat nodded and tripped away
I have tailed
These banal clerks of mass murder
Bayers of blood
Passing themselves off as judge and jury
Deep into their
Wine-soaked orgies where flush
With self-congratulation
They hammer and stammer at tables
Eyes ablaze mouths
Laughing at tomorrow's foregone conclusions
Amid their songs
And laughter women slide under their fingers
Put tongues in their
Laughing mouths a whole troupe of them
Who had loved the drowned
Twist in the beds of their lovers' killers
For greed or glory
These spoils of war are weak and dazzled
By the spell of power of
Death bestowed or stayed by hungry kisses
Skirts slither
Down blouses spill at the least touch
Of ink-stained fingers
Remorse they say is the currency of all sins
But what remorse eats
At the liver pollutes the sleep of these
Troughers of blood
Who can do justice to the horrors
Perpetrated by such
Slouching monsters sure you might lance the boil
But drown in pus.

La Jeune Captive[16]

'L'épi naissant mûrit de la faux respecté;
Sans crainte du pressoir, le pampre tout l'été
     Boit les doux présents de l'aurore;
Et moi, comme lui belle, et jeune comme lui,
Quoi que l'heure présente ait de trouble et d'ennui,
     Je ne veux point mourir encore.

Qu'un stoïque aux yeux secs vole embrasser la mort:
Moi je pleure et j'espère. Au noir souffle du nord
     Je plie et relève ma tête.
S'il est des jours amers, il en est de si doux!
Hélas! quel miel jamais n'a laissé de dégoûts?
     Quelle mer n'a point de tempête?

L'illusion féconde habite dans mon sein.
D'une prison sur moi les murs pèsent en vain,
     J'ai les ailes de l'espérance.
Échappée aux réseaux de l'oiseleur cruel,
Plus vive, plus heureuse, aux campagnes du ciel
     Philomèle chante et s'élance.

Est-ce à moi de mourir? Tranquille je m'endors
Et tranquille je veille; et ma veille aux remords
     Ni mon sommeil ne sont en proie.
Ma bienvenue au jour me rit dans tous les yeux;
Sur des fronts abattus, mon aspect dans ces lieux
     Ranime presque de la joie.

Mon beau voyage encore est si loin de sa fin!
Je pars, et des ormeaux qui bordent le chemin
     J'ai passé les premiers à peine,
Au banquet de la vie à peine commencé,
Un instant seulement mes lèvres ont pressé
     La coupe en mes mains encor pleine.

Je ne suis qu'au printemps, je veux voir la moisson,
Et comme le soleil, de saison en saison,
     Je veux achever mon année.
Brillante sur ma tige et l'honneur du jardin,
Je n'ai vu luire encor que les feux du matin;
     Je veux achever ma journée.

Young Woman Imprisoned

'No rash sickle lays low the budding wheat,
No zealous flail threshes the summer heat
From the dew-swollen rye.
And I, just as golden, just as youthful,
Despite these days of turmoil and trouble,
I don't want to die.

Dry-eyed stoics might lightly smile on death.
I? — I hope and cry. The north wind's black breath
Buffets me but will pass.
If some days are bitter, other still are sweet.
What honey doesn't cloy with sick surfeit?
What sea is smooth as glass?

My mind feeds daily on fresh illusion.
Walls buckle and fall in sweet confusion.
Hope buoys my outspread wings,
As when the lark slips the cruel bird-catcher's nets
And, jubilant then, exultantly jets
Into the sky and sings.

Am I to die? I who calmly fall asleep,
Who calmly wake — nor waking hours nor sleep
A prey to listless guilt.
My presence even prompts a glad surprise,
Stirs soft smiles, restores life to death-dulled eyes,
To words a kindly lilt.

I've just begun life's beautiful journey —
Just stepped beneath the dappling canopy
Of the elm-lined road ahead!
At life's feast, far from having supped all up,
My lips have barely kissed the brimful cup,
And whet my thirst instead.

I'm in my springtime, yet still want to see
The harvest in, then like the sun swing smoothly
Through the declining year.
As a bloom that's barely seen dawn's first light yet,
I long to feel noon blaze, then warm sunset
Dwindle to an ember.

O mort! tu peux attendre; éloigne, éloigne-toi;
Va consoler les cœurs que la honte, l'effroi,
    Le pâle désespoir dévore.
Pour moi Palès encore a des asiles verts,
Les Amours des baisers, les Muses des concerts.
    Je ne veux point mourir encore.'

Ainsi, triste et captif, ma lyre toutefois
S'éveillait, écoutant ces plaintes, cette voix,
    Ces vœux d'une jeune captive;
Et secouant le faix de mes jours languissants,
Aux douces lois des vers je pliai les accents
    De sa bouche aimable et naïve.

Ces chants, de ma prison témoins harmonieux,
Feront à quelque amant des loisirs studieux
    Chercher quelle fut cette belle.
La grâce décorait son front et ses discours,
Et comme elle craindront de voir finir leurs jours
    Ceux qui les passeront près d'elle.

Ah! death, hold off a while, don't come so near;
Go comfort hearts consumed by shame, by fear,
By pale despair bled dry.
In the green meadows yet I'll know what peace is,
What raptures are in art, in lovers' kisses —
I don't want to die.'

Listening to her wistful, wishful reverie
A lyric impulse would awake in me,
Though sad and captive too.
Shedding then the languor of my own eclipse,
I set to verse the words slipped from the lips
Of this lovely ingénue.

These few lines scanning our shared cell in rhyme
Will likewise mark some idling lover's time
Who seeks this beauty out.
And they will fear for their own lives who pace
Her cell and sigh with her, whose form was grace,
Whose fate was mortal doubt.

Ils vivent cependant et de tant de victimes[17]

Ils vivent cependant et de tant de victimes
    Les cris ne montent pas vers toi.
C'est un pauvre poète, ô grand Dieu des armées,
    Qui seul, captif, près de la mort,
Attachant à ses vers les ailes enflammées
    De ton tonnerre qui s'endort,
De la vertu proscrite embrassant la défense,
    Dénonce aux juges infernaux
Ces juges, ces jurés qui frappent l'innocence,
    Hécatombe à leurs tribunaux.
Eh bien, fais-moi donc vivre, et cette horde impure
    Sentira quels traits sont les miens.
Ils ne sont point cachés dans leur bassesse obscure:
    Je les vois, j'accours, je les tiens.
Sur ses pieds inégaux l'épode vengeresse
    Saura les atteindre pourtant.
Diamant ceint d'azur, Paros, œil de la Grèce,
    De l'onde Égée astre éclatant,
Dans tes flancs où Nature est sans cesse à l'ouvrage,
    Pour le ciseau laborieux
Vit et blanchit le marbre illustre de l'image
    Et des grands hommes et des Dieux.
Mais pour graver aussi la honte ineffaçable,
    Paros de l'ïambe acéré
Aiguisa le burin brûlant, impérissable.
    Fils d'Archiloque, fier André,
Ne détends point ton arc, fléau de l'imposture.
    Que des passants pleins de tes vers,
Les siècles, l'avenir, que toute la nature
    Crie à l'aspect de ces pervers:
Hou, les vils scélérats! les monstres! les infâmes!
    De vol, de massacres nourris,
Noirs ivrognes de sang, lâches bourreaux des femmes
    Qui n'égorgent point leurs maris;
Du fils tendre et pieux; et du malheureux père
    Pleurant son fils assassiné;
Du frère qui n'a point laissé dans la misère
    Périr son frère abandonné.
Vous n'avez qu'une vie... ô vampires...
    Et vous n'expierez qu'une fois
Tant de morts et de pleurs, de cendres, de décombres,
    Qui contre vous lèvent la voix!

That They Live and Their Numberless Victims' Anguish

That they live and their numberless victims' anguish
Be a voice crying in the vastness,
O great Lord of hosts, of your indifference,
A poor poet uprises
And though he be in chains, near death and friendless,
Lets the lightning you relinquish
Course through his verse that keenly embraces
Virtue banished and denounces
Our vile magistrates and their baying juries
To yet more infernal judges.
Just let me slip their bloody assizes
To show this filth that I mean business.
They're not hidden by their murky meanness:
I see them, seize them, and thus
The hastening-halting feet of this verse
Will have them none the less.
A diamond encrusted in azure, Paros,
Coruscating eye of Greece,
Winks in the sky-blue Aegean where ceaseless
Nature feeds the sculptor's artifice
With a marble of such stunning whiteness
It breathes great men and gods' likeness.
Yet Paros also whet to steely keenness
A chisel of iambic verse
With which to score shame indelible and deathless.
Proud André, son to Archilochus,
Don't let your whip-hand falter — it's imposture's scourge.
Let onlookers, fired with your verse,
Let centuries past and to come, let nature curse
The sight of these corrupt creatures:
— Hoo, a curse on you, vile dogs! loathsome worms! monsters!
Fatted on slaughter, theft and vice,
Blind drunk on blood, butchers, cowardly and vicious,
Of whole unfortunate families —
Of tender, godly sons, wives direly loyal to spouses,
Fathers grieving their murdered boys,
Of brothers unwilling to leave brothers otherwise
Dumped to rot in gutters.
You have only one life, blood-suckers...
And will expiate but once
So many deaths and tears, rubble and ashes
Which damn you in shrill chorus!

J'ai lu qu'un batelier[18]

J'ai lu qu'un batelier, entrant dans sa nacelle,
 Jetait à l'eau son aviron.
J'ai lu qu'un écuyer noble et fier sur la selle,
 Bien armé d'un double éperon,
D'abord ôtait la bride à son coursier farouche.
 J'ai lu qu'un sage renommé,
Avant de s'endormir, dans le fond de sa couche
 Plaçait un tison allumé.
J'ai lu que, pour franchir des routes difficiles,
 Un Automédon pétulant
Enlevait les écrous des quatre orbes agiles
 Qui roulaient sous son char brillant.
J'ai lu qu'un Actéon à son tour sur l'arène
 Assouvit la rage et la faim
De ses chiens, par lui seul, pour bien servir sa h[aine],
 Accoutumés au sang humain.
[L'Automédon meurtri devint un Hippolyte.
 Le sage...
...l'écuyer à pied descendit à Cocyte.
 Le nocher...
Un sot enfant jouait avec des grains de poudre.][19]
 ...

Un docte à grands projets rassembla des vip[ères]
 Et leur prêchait fraternité.
Mais déchiré bientôt par ce peuple de frères,
 Il dit: 'Je l'ai bien mérité.
Un seul de ces serpents qui se cache sous l'herbe
 Est terrible; et moi...
Je les réunis tous. Je joins... superbe
 Et l'audace aux mauvais penchants.'
J'ai lu maints autres faits, tous fort bons à redire,
 Et tous ces beaux faits que j'ai lus,
Barnave, Chapelier, Duport les devaient lire.
 Ceux-ci ne lisent pas non plus.

I Read About a Rower

I read about a rower getting in his boat
Who promptly threw his oars in the water.

I read about a jockey getting on his mount
Who promptly undid both reins and halter.

And the great philosopher I read about
Who used a burning log for a bolster.

And the racing driver heading out off-road
Who loosed every wheel-nut on his sports car.

I read about a huntsman whose dogs scented blood
Who then served himself up to their hunger.

[...]

A bookish sort dreamed aloud of brotherhood
Before a coalescing nest of vipers.

They most fraternally tore him apart,
Although he owned: 'I deserve no better.

Just one of these snakes in the grass is bad
Enough. And I brought them all together.'

And lots of other facts I read about
Lots of folk would do well to mull them over.

Tolerant, reasoning men were bound
To read them. They don't read any longer.

Mon frère, que jamais la tristesse importune[20]

Mon f[rère,] que jamais la tristesse importune
        Ne trouble ses prospérités!
Qu'il remplisse à la fois la scène et la tribune!
        Que les grandeurs et la fortune
Le comblent de leurs biens qu'il a tant souhaités!

Que les Muses, les arts, toujours d'un nouveau lustre
        Embellissent tous ses travaux;
Et que, cédant à peine à son vingtième lustre,
        De son tombeau la pierre illustre
S'élève radieuse entre tous les tombeaux!

Mais...
        Infortune, honnêtes douleurs,
Souffrance, des vertus superbe et chaste fille,
        Salut. Mes frères, ma famille,
Sont tous les opprimés, ceux qui versent des pleurs,

Ceux que livre à la hache un féroce caprice;
        Ceux qui brûlent un noble encens
Aux pieds de la vertu que l'on traîne au supplice,
        Et bravent le sceptre du vice,
Ses caresses, ses dons, ses regards menaçants;

Ceux qui devant le crime, idole ensanglantée,
        N'ont jamais fléchi les genoux,
Et soudain, à sa vue impie et détestée,
        Sentent leur poitrine agitée,
Et s'enflammer leur front d'un généreux courroux.

I Wish My Brother to Flourish Forever

I wish my brother to flourish forever
And never know cruel luck!
Let the publics of parliament and theatre
Acclaim his every work!
That he bask in the glory he's longed for!

Let fresh inspiration give to his art
Ever more beauty and brilliance,
That a hundred years hence if this fine heart
Succumb, a stele shall be raised
More splendid than all other monuments!

And yet...
Welcome also misfortune,
Welcome grief and the pain that arises
From obdurate opposition
To crime. Such a rule oppresses

Now my family who stand for all others
Oppressed, all those offered up
To the guillotine on the whim of monsters;
The steadfast who refuse to stoop
To the blandishments and threats of butchers;

They have never knelt, and will not kneel now,
To the blood-stained idol worshipped
By murderers and crooks. Appalled at the view,
Rare anger wells and, as if slapped,
A pale rage flares proudly across cheek and brow.

On vit; on vit infâme[21]

On vit; on vit infâme. Eh bien? il fallut l'être;
    L'infâme après tout mange et dort.
Ici même, en ses parcs, où la mort nous fait paître,
    Où la hache nous tire au sort,
Beaux poulets sont écrits; maris, amants sont dupes;
    Caquetage, intrigue de sots.
On y chante; on y joue; on y lève des jupes;
    On y fait chansons et bons mots;
L'un pousse et fait bondir sur les toits, sur les vitres,
    Un ballon tout gonflé de vent,
Comme sont les discours de sept cents plats bélî[tres],
    Dont Barère et le plus savant.
L'autre court; l'autre saute; et braillent, boivent, rient,
    Politiqueurs et raisonneurs;
Et sur les gonds de fer soudain les portes cri[ent].
    Des juges tigres nos seigneurs
Le pourvoyeur paraît. Quelle sera la proie
    Que la hache appelle aujourd'hui?
Chacun frissonne, écoute; et chacun avec joie
    Voit que ce n'est pas encor lui:
Ce sera toi demain, insensible imbécile.

We Live; We Live Loathsome

We live; we live loathsome. So? We had no choice:
The loathsome too must sleep and eat.
In these very holding-pens where death corrals us,
As the blade picks which throat to slit,
Here *billets doux* are penned; husbands, lovers, cheated.
Chitter-chatter, fools conspiring.
Songs are sung; games are played; skirts lifted;
Witty things said, impromptu choiring;
Someone flicks a balloon against the rafters
And panes, a round ball of hot air,
Like the speeches of seven hundred shysters,
None smarter than Cit'zen Barère.
Someone runs, someone skips; and laughing, braying,
drinking,
Others split hairs, spout politics;
Till suddenly, its iron hinges shrieking,
The door reveals the slick
Expediter sent by our fierce lord-judges. Who'll
Then be the blade's next victim?
Each of us shudders, listens; and each, gleeful,
Sees that it's not yet him.
Tomorrow, unfeeling dolt, your turn will come.[22]

Quand au mouton bêlant la sombre boucherie[23]

Quand au mouton bêlant la sombre boucherie
        Ouvre ses cavernes de mort,
Pâtres, chiens et moutons, toute la bergerie
        Ne s'informe plus de son sort.
Les enfants qui suivaient ses ébats dans la plaine,
        Les vierges aux belles couleurs
Qui le baisaient en foule et sur sa blanche laine
        Entrelaçaient rubans et fleurs,
Sans plus penser à lui le mangent s'il est tendre.
        Dans cet abîme enseveli
J'ai le même destin. Je m'y devais attendre.
        Accoutumons-nous à l'oubli.
Oubliés comme moi dans cet affreux repaire,
        Mille autres moutons, comme moi,
Pendus aux crocs sanglants du charnier populaire,
        Seront servis au peuple roi.
Que pouvaient mes amis? Oui, de leur main chérie
        Un mot à travers ces barreaux
Eût versé quelque baume en mon âme flétrie;
        De l'or peut-être à mes bourreaux...
Mais tout est précipice. Ils ont le droit de vivre.
        Vivez, amis; vivez contents.
En dépit de... soyez lents à me suivre.
        Peut-être en de plus heureux temps
J'ai moi-même, à l'aspect des pleurs de l'infort[une],
        Détourné mes regards distraits.
A mon tour aujourd'hui mon malheur importune.
        Vivez, amis; vivez en paix.

Opening Like a Maw the Dark Abattoir

Opening like a maw the dark abattoir
Greets the bleating sheep
While shepherd, dog and flock, the whole sorry lot,
Look on with not a peep.
Boys who gambolled with lambs in the meadows,
Girls, all sugar and spice,
Who'd deck white fleeces with ribbons and kisses,
Now, without thinking twice,
Enjoy their lamb tender — to carve and eat.
It's now perfectly obvious.
My fate's the lambs' fate: swallowed up in this pit
And the world oblivious.
Like me a thousand other sheep languish
In this foul hole forgotten,
Each hooked and bleeding in the people's meatshop —
King Mob must have his mutton.
What could my friends do? Their dear hand might indeed
Have poured a little balm
On my shrunk soul with a word slipped through the bars;
Gold to grease a gaoler's palm...
But we all toe the abyss. They got to live.
So live, friends; live happy.
Spite the hangman and be slow to take my lead.
In happier times maybe
I too have looked away from desperate tears,
Distracted; my miseries
In turn now are ill-timed and bothersome.
Live, my friends; live in peace.

Comme un dernier rayon[24]

Comme un dernier rayon, comme un dernier zéphy[re]
    Animent la fin d'un beau jour,
Au pied de l'échafaud j'essaye encor ma lyre.
    Peut-être est-ce bientôt mon tour.
Peut-être avant que l'heure en cercle promenée
    Ait posé sur l'émail brillant,
Dans les soixante pas où sa route est bornée,
    Son pied sonore et vigilant;
Le sommeil du tombeau pressera ma paupière.
    Avant que de ses deux moitiés
Ce vers que je commence ait atteint la dernière,
    Peut-être en ces murs effrayés
Le messager de mort, noir recruteur des ombres,
    Escorté d'infâmes soldats,
Ébranlant de mon nom ces longs corridors sombres,
    Où seul dans la foule à grands pas
J'erre, aiguisant ces dards persécuteurs du crime,
    Du juste trop faibles soutiens,
Sur mes lèvres soudain va suspendre la rime;
    Et chargeant mes bras de liens,
Me traîner, amassant en foule à mon passage
    Mes tristes compagnons reclus,
Qui me connaissaient tous avant l'affreux message,
    Mais qui ne me connaissent plus.
Eh bien! j'ai trop vécu. Quelle franchise auguste,
    De mâle constance et d'honneur
Quels exemples sacrés, doux à l'âme du juste,
    Pour lui quelle ombre de bonheur,
Quelle Thémis terrible aux têtes criminelles,
    Quels pleurs d'une noble pitié,
Des antiques bienfaits quels souvenirs fidèles,
    Quels beaux échanges d'amitié,
Font digne de regrets l'habitacle des hommes?
    La peur fugitive est leur Dieu;
La bassesse; la feinte. Ah! lâches que nous sommes
    Tous, oui, tous. Adieu, terre, adieu.
Vienne, vienne la mort! — Que la mort me délivre!
    Ainsi donc mon cœur abattu
Cède au poids de ses maux? Non, non. Puissé-je vivre!
    Ma vie importe à la vertu.
Car l'honnête homme enfin, victime de l'outrage,
    Dans les cachots, près du cercueil,

As One Last Soft Breeze

As one last soft breeze, one last beam of light
Freshen a rosy sky
So on the gallows-step my voice rings clear and light,
Though my turn comes by and by.
Before perhaps the present hour is out
Across the bright enamel dial
The clock-hand will still be marking out
A sure and sonorous meanwhile
Though death's sleep some time since has closed my eyes.
Within perhaps these frightened walls
My pen will leave then t's uncrossed, undotted i's,
When death's messenger calls,
A harvester of souls knocking at the doors,
And with him men without shame
Making the long lugubrious corridors
Echo harshly to my name,
Their voice freezing on my lips a bitter rhyme
All set to obliterate
These same criminals, though their thriving crime
Is little troubled by my hate;
Then quickly cuffed and chained, my wretched cellmates
Judging me (so the condemned condemn),
Fellow-feeling snuffed in former intimates
Strange to me now — I dead to them.
So then! I've lived too long. What after all
Would make this world a loss
Worth mourning? Where's the honesty in all
These fine people? The love across
The years inspiring kindness, friendship?
Where's the implacable justice
That blasts the wicked and offers kinship
With the oppressed? Here there just is
A cabal of crooks holding unending sway...
Fear, fleeting fear, grips us all.
Cheating, despicable, each in his own way
A little coward. Let's call
An end to this. Let death come now and take me!
Is this then how my abject mind
Would buckle under its pain and break me?
No! Let me live and living find
An outraged voice to serve the common good,
And though sunk in this dank berth

Relève plus altiers son front et son langage,
 Brillants d'un généreux orgueil.
S'il est écrit aux cieux que jamais une épée
 N'étincellera dans mes mains;
Dans l'encre et l'amertume une autre arme trempée
 Peut encor servir les humains.
Justice, Vérité, si ma main, si ma bouche,
 Si mes pensers les plus secrets
Ne froncèrent jamais votre sourcil farouche,
 Et si les infâmes progrès,
Si la risée atroce, ou, plus atroce injure,
 L'encens de hideux scélérats
Ont pénétré vos cœurs d'une longue blessure;
 Sauvez-moi. Conservez un bras
Qui lance votre foudre, un amant qui vous venge.
 Mourir sans vider mon carq[uois]!
Sans percer, sans fouler, sans pétrir dans leur fan[ge]
 Ces bourreaux barbouilleurs de lois!
Ces vers cadavéreux de la France asservie,
 Égorgée! O mon cher trésor,
O ma plume! fiel, bile, horreur, Dieux de ma vie!
 Par vous seuls je respire encor:
Comme la poix brûlante agitée en ses veines
 Ressuscite un flambeau mourant,
Je souffre; mais je vis. Par vous, loin de mes peines,
 D'espérance un vaste torrent
Me transporte. Sans vous, comme un poison livide,
 L'invisible dent du chagrin,
Mes amis opprimés, du menteur homicide
 Les succès, le sceptre d'airain;
Des bons proscrits par lui la mort ou la ruine,
 L'opprobre de subir sa loi,
Tout eût tari ma vie; ou contre ma poitrine
 Dirigé mon poignard. Mais quoi!
Nul ne resterait donc pour attendrir l'histoire
 Sur tant de justes massacrés?
Pour consoler leurs fils, leurs veuves, leur mém[oire],
 Pour que des brigands abhorrés
Frémissent aux portraits noirs de leur ressemblance,
 Pour descendre jusqu'aux enfers
Nouer le triple fouet, le fouet de la vengeance
 Déjà levé sur ces pervers?
Pour cracher sur leurs noms, pour chanter leur supplice?
 Allons, étouffe tes clameurs;
Souffre, ô cœur gros de haine, affamé de justice.
 Toi, Vertu, pleure si je meurs.

And close to death, rise up for all that's good
And just and fair on earth.
If it's decreed I'll never raise a sword
To rain steel on my vicious foes,
I can still wage war with each envenomed word,
Each pen-thrust eviscerating those
Who make a mockery of justice, truth,
Who bathe in grossest flattery,
Urging uncouth sneers and yet more uncouth
Slander; yet if I may be
Considered worthy of the cause, spare me now!
I might then take my courage
In both hands to strike a fatal blow
Against this vile regime, to rage
Against these weasel-men who daub their laws in blood,
To empty a full magazine
In the bloated gut of this false brotherhood
Feasting on France. Taste my spleen!
See how my pen is steeped in it, how bile
And bitterness keep me alive.
My pain feeds me as a dash of volatile
Oils helps an ebbing fire revive.
Strange how this anger's a well-spring of hope
Buoying me up beyond
The grief. Without it there's no stomach to cope
With infamies heaped on friends, and
Good people butchered or bust by sordid
Men, sure in their power, whose rule
Distils a venom that eats like acid
At my heart — a hurt so cruel
That without this thirst in me for justice
I'd have long since slit my throat.
And what then? Who would bear witness to this
Havoc or make less remote
The sheer horror of our times? Who will console
The legions of the bereft?
Who will show these monsters their own monstrous soul
Blackened with vice? Who will be left
To spit on their graves or pursue these fiends
Through hellfire? But I waste my breath.
I'll tend instead to my hate-filled heart. Friends
Of the truth, weep, weep at my death.

Notes

1. The base text for all of Chénier's poems here is his *Œuvres complètes*, ed. by Walter. I am very grateful to the Éditions Gallimard for permission to reproduce the poems from this edition. I will also reference here, where appropriate, the widely used *Poésies*, ed. by Louis Becq de Fouquières (Paris: Gallimard, 1994), a facsimile reproduction of the 'Édition Critique' of 1872. For the 'Hymne' above, see *Œuvres complètes*, pp. 164–66; *Poésies*, pp. cxx–cxxiii. The title here of the 'Hymne' reproduces that of its original publication in *Journal de Paris*, 15 April 1792. The order of the poems, as presented here, is broadly chronological.
2. *Œuvres complètes*, p. 187; *Poésies*, pp. 453–54.
3. *Œuvres complètes*, pp. 88–89; *Poésies*, p. 119.
4. *Œuvres complètes*, p. 546; *Poésies*, pp. 286–87.
5. *Œuvres complètes*, pp. 119–20; *Poésies*, pp. 289–90.
6. *Œuvres complètes*, p. 117; *Poésies*, pp. 292–93.
7. *Œuvres complètes*, pp. 178–80; *Poésies*, pp. 455–58.
8. *Œuvres complètes*, pp. 404–05; *Poésies*, pp. 385–86.
9. *Œuvres complètes*, pp. 565–66; *Poésies*, pp. 452–53.
10. *Œuvres complètes*, p. 183; *Poésies*, pp. 447–48.
11. *Œuvres complètes*, pp. 183–85; *Poésies*, pp. 299–301.
12. *Œuvres complètes*, pp. 187–89.
13. *Œuvres complètes*, pp. 181–83; *Poésies*, pp. 448–51.
14. *Œuvres complètes*, p. 189.
15. *Œuvres complètes*, p. 191.
16. *Œuvres complètes*, pp. 185–86; *Poésies*, pp. 462–66.
17. *Œuvres complètes*, pp. 189–90. This text is presented as two distinct poems in the *Œuvres complètes* but, following the argument of Francis Scarfe, it is given here as a single section of verse. See Chénier, *Poems*, pp. 141–42.
18. *Œuvres complètes*, p. 571.
19. This unfinished section is too fragmentary to translate as part of the poem. It broadly reads: 'The bruised driver was crushed to death. | The wise man... | ... The horseman went on foot into the underworld. | The boatman... | A foolish child toyed with gunpowder'.
20. *Œuvres complètes*, pp. 567–68; *Poésies*, p. 446, only giving the first ten lines.
21. *Œuvres complètes*, pp. 192–93.
22. See also the brilliant translation of this poem by Tom Paulin, 'From the Death Cell', in *The Road to Inver: Translations, Versions, Imitations 1975–2003* (London: Faber & Faber, 2004), p. 19; and the equally fascinating analysis of it in Scott, *The Work of Literary Translation*, pp. 114–18.
23. *Œuvres complètes*, p. 192; *Poésies*, pp. 467–69.
24. *Œuvres complètes*, pp. 193–95; *Poésies*, pp. 467, 469–71. There are a number of significant differences in the version of this poem in *Poésies* from that given in the *Œuvres complètes*.

GLOSSARY OF
NAMES AND PLACES

❖

A

Actéon (Actaeon). A Theban hero and legendary hunter who fatally incurred the wrath of Artemis, the Greek goddess of the hunt, of wild animals and chastity. Actaeon surprised the goddess bathing naked with her women attendants so, as punishment, she transformed him into a stag whereupon he was torn to pieces by his own hounds.

Alcide (Alcides). Another name for Heracles.

Apollo. Son of Zeus and twin brother to Artemis, Apollo is the Greek god of music, poetry, dance, prophecy and truth, health and healing, animal husbandry and youth. He is also the god of archery and at only four days old, he took up his bow and arrow to slay the monstrous serpent Python, violating the sacred shrine at Delphi to do so.

Archiloque (Archilochus). A seventh-century BCE Greek lyric poet from the island of Paros (see Paros). He was famous as a poet of censure and blame, often using obscene or violent satirical language. He largely composed iambic verse, that is, verse consisting of a short/long or weak/strong or unstressed/stressed measure. His invectives were so powerful and shaming that they allegedly drove his former fiancée and her father to suicide (see Lycambe). At the end of his 'Voûtes du Panthéon', Chénier styles himself as 'le citoyen Archiloque Mastigophore', or 'citizen Archilochus wielder of the scourge or whip'.

Argonautes (Argonauts). A crew of fifty ancient Greek heroes who sailed from Iolcus in Thessaly under the command of Jason in his ship the Argo. They travelled to distant Colchis in order to steal the Golden Fleece and retrieve the unburied ghost of one of Jason's distant relatives, Phrixus. After many adventures, they succeeded in their task and returned to Thessaly.

Atlas. According to Greek mythology, after the Titans were defeated by the Olympian gods, the Titan Atlas was condemned by Zeus to stand on the western edge of the Earth and hold up the sky on his shoulder.

Automédon (Automedon). Achilles's charioteer in the Trojan War.

B

Bacchanales, Les (Bacchanalia). Religious festivals celebrated in Antiquity, most notably in Rome. They were held in honour of the Roman god Bacchus (in

Greek, Dionysus), god of ritual madness and ecstasy, intoxication, wine and fecundity. The Roman festivals lasted between three to five days and were notorious for their drunken and sexual licence.

Barère de Vieuzac, Bertrand. An eloquent lawyer from Toulouse, Barère was elected to the Estates-General in 1789 and became a representative in the first National Assembly. He served as a judge from October 1791 until September 1792 when he was elected to the National Convention. He was presiding officer of the Convention during the trial of Louis XVI and voted for the king's death. He joined the Committee of Public Safety in April 1793 and was one of only two members to serve during its entire existence. He became the Committee's principal spokesman in the Convention through the Terror (1793–94) and it is in this role that Chénier often viciously attacks him for his bombastic justifications of political violence and arbitrary rule couched in high-sounding revolutionary jargon. Barère championed a political cult of nationalism that allowed him to shift between factions, siding against Robespierre and his followers in the parliamentary coup of July 1794 (so-called Thermidor). Nonetheless, he was tainted by association with the Terror and was imprisoned in 1795. On hearing that he was to be tried and most probably guillotined, he escaped from prison and went into hiding in Bordeaux. When Bonaparte took power in 1799, Barère served the new regime as a secret agent. The Bourbon Restoration exiled him from France as a regicide. He lived in Brussels until 1830 after which he returned to France. He died in 1841, aged eighty-five, the last surviving member of the Committee of Public Safety, leaving behind him important, if partisan, memoirs.

Barnave, Antoine-Joseph-Marie-Pierre. A Protestant lawyer from Grenoble, Barnave became one of the most influential orators of the National Assembly in the early Revolution (1789–91). A member of the Jacobin Club until it split over the king's escape attempt of June 1791, Barnave helped to found the more conservative Feuillant Club. His moderate constitutional monarchism was close to Chénier's own political stance. Barnave opposed the war with Austria in 1792 but his influence was already on the wane. He was arrested in Grenoble after the overthrow of the monarchy in August 1792. The discovery of his secret correspondence with Marie-Antoinette contributed to his fate when he was eventually transferred to Paris for trial in November 1793. He was found guilty of treason and guillotined on 29 November 1793.

Boötes. A constellation in the northern sky. The name comes from the Greek for 'ox-driver'.

Bourdon, Léonard. Having studied law in Orléans, Bourdon moved to Paris in the 1780s to promote educational reform. He was elected to the Estates-General in 1789 and joined the Jacobin Club the following year. After the fall of the monarchy, he was elected to the Convention and is caricatured by Chénier as a blood-thirsty demagogue close to Marat. Bourdon fell out with Robespierre in 1794 and so survived Thermidor, although he was arrested in April 1795 and imprisoned in northern France. On his release later the same year, he undertook a number of administrative and diplomatic roles for subsequent revolutionary and imperial regimes. He died in 1807.

Brissot, Jacques-Pierre. A reformist writer and radical journalist, exiled in London in the 1780s, Brissot was also an early abolitionist. At the outbreak of the Revolution, he returned to Paris and edited the influential news-sheet *Le Patriote français* (1789–93). A vocal member of the Jacobin Club in 1791–92, Brissot was elected to the Legislative Assembly and its successor, the Convention. He was a notable proponent of war against Austria and Prussia and allied himself with the federalist republicans known as the Girondins. It is as a war-mongering journalist, overt republican and influential Jacobin that Brissot was attacked personally by Chénier in 1792 in the rival moderate news-sheet the *Journal de Paris*. Nonetheless, Brissot opposed Louis XVI's execution and fell under the suspicion of more radical revolutionaries. He was purged from the Convention and arrested with his Girondin allies on 2 June 1793. Brissot was tried with the Girondins and they were collectively sentenced to death and guillotined on 31 October 1793.

Byzance (Byzantium). Byzantium is the name of an important Greek colony in Antiquity situated on the Bosphorus where the river forms a strait between the Black Sea and the Sea of Marmara. At the end of the second century CE, it became a major Roman city and the emperor Constantine made it an imperial residence in 330. After the emperor's death, the city was renamed Constantinople in his honour and became the capital of the Byzantine or Eastern Roman Empire until it was overrun by the Ottomans in 1453. The Ottomans subsequently made the city their capital. Chénier was born in Constantinople in the suburb of Galata in 1762. His mother was Greek, so the Greek name for the Ottoman capital provided the poet with a mythical lineage via his birthplace back to ancient Rome and Greece. However, the poetic colouring of the ode 'A Byzance' is heavily orientalist, rather than neo-classical, and it was allegedly inspired by a passage in Voltaire's *Histoire de Charles XII* about the early eighteenth-century sultan Ahmed III.

C

Cabanis, Pierre-Jean-Georges. A physician by training and a freemason before 1789, Cabanis became an advocate and practitioner of hospital reform in the early Revolution. He was Mirabeau's personal doctor during the revolutionary's last illness in March-April 1791 and wrote a detailed account of it. Like Chénier, Cabanis was a member of the moderate club La Société de 1789. He was also a friend of the poet Roucher who was a fellow freemason and who would share Chénier's fate in July 1794. Cabanis is cited in Chénier's iambics 'Voûtes du Panthéon' most probably because his account of Mirabeau's last hours offers an enlightened contrast to the clamorous hagiography surrounding Marat's death. Despite his relatively conservative politics, Cabanis survived the Terror, seemingly as a result of his work in the hospitals of the regime and his sustained efforts on behalf of poor relief. Despite supporting Bonaparte's *coup d'état* in November 1799, he opposed the authoritarian direction of the regime and devoted himself instead to his vitalist-materialist philosophy and to an early form of evolutionary physiology. Cabanis died in 1808. Ironically, given his place in Chénier's poem, he was buried in the Panthéon, with his funeral oration delivered by Garat.

Calvados, Le. One of five new *départements* created out of the old region of Normandy by the revolutionary regime in March 1790, Le Calvados was, and still is, centred on the city of Caen. In mid-1793 it was one of many *départements* that rose up against the centralized Jacobin state and its drive to expand the war effort and conscript more soldiers. It associated itself particularly with the federalist *députés* of the so-called Gironde, many of whom attempted to flee to Caen after their eviction from the Convention and indictment by forces loyal to the Jacobins. It was also from Caen that the young Charlotte Corday set out to assassinate Jean-Paul Marat in July 1793.

Carrier, Jean-Baptiste. Elected to the Convention in September 1792, Carrier was also a member of the popular Jacobin and Cordelier Clubs. As a *représentant-en-mission*, or elected representative seconded outside Paris to oversee the war effort, Carrier was sent to Nantes in October 1793. He rounded up all suspected counter-revolutionaries and, with a gang of local henchmen called the 'Marat Company', he had many suspects summarily guillotined or shot. As the prisons filled, Carrier oversaw the mass drowning of between 1,800 and 4,000 men, women and children in the Loire river between November 1793 and January 1794. When news of his excesses reached Paris, Carrier was recalled to the capital. After the fall of Robespierre and his followers in July 1794, Carrier was arrested in September and denounced for his crimes in Nantes. He was actively scapegoated by other former Terrorist *représentants-en-mission*, tried, found guilty and unanimously sentenced to death. He was guillotined on 16 December 1794.

Cathay. An early modern European name for northern China. By the eighteenth century, its use was largely poetic.

Caton (Cato the Younger). Marcus Porcius Cato Uticensis was a first-century BCE senator in the late Roman republic. He was renowned for his elevated oratory and moral integrity in a period of widespread corruption. He committed suicide rather than submit to Julius Caesar's rule after the latter's victory in the Roman civil war. He is used by Chénier as an obvious satirical foil for the grandiose rhetoric and venal politics of certain mediocre *députés* in the Convention.

Chabot, François. A Capuchin friar from Rodez who embraced the Revolution and became a constitutional priest in 1790, Chabot was elected to both the Legislative National Assembly and the National Convention. In the latter, he voted for the king's death and in March 1793 he was sent out to quell counter-revolutionary revolts, first in the Aveyron region, then in Toulouse, which he did with zeal and brutality. Compromised in financial speculations in November 1793, his case was aggravated by his marriage to the wealthy daughter of an Austrian-Jewish banker. Chabot was tried and executed with Georges-Jacques Danton and his political allies on 5 April 1794, although the Dantonists, as they were called, refused all association with such a 'scoundrel'.

Chapelier. See Le Chapelier.

Chénier, Marie-Joseph-Blaise. André Chénier's younger brother (*b.* 1764). See the Biography of André Chénier for details of his life and works, particularly where they impinge on his elder brother's life and works.

Cloots, Anacharsis. Jean-Baptiste du Val-de-Grâce, baron de Cloots (also spelt Clootz). An extremely wealthy Prussian nobleman, Cloots was educated in Paris, travelled widely, and was inspired by progressive ideals. He embraced the Revolution and presented himself at the bar of the National Assembly in June 1790 as the spokesman for a delegation of foreigners swearing allegiance on behalf of 'humankind' to the revolutionary Rights of Man and the Citizen. Thereafter he dropped his noble title and took up the name of Anacharsis in honour of Jean-Jacques Barthélemy's famous philosophical romance set in ancient Athens, *Le Voyage du jeune Anacharsis en Grèce* (1788). In 1792 he supported and personally funded the war effort and the overthrow of the monarchy. He became a French citizen, a representative in the National Convention and voted for the death of Louis XVI. Chénier, who spells his name 'Clotz', pronounced 'Cloh' to rhyme with Laclos, cites him as another misguided but insufficiently vicious eulogist for Marat's funeral rites. However, by late 1793, as a wealthy foreigner in a time of war, Cloots was excluded from the Jacobin Club and was viewed with increasing suspicion by hard-line revolutionaries. Although patently innocent, the Prussian was enlisted as 'proof' of a foreign plot in the indictment of the atheist extremists grouped around the journalist Jacques-René Hébert. He was condemned and executed with so-called Hébertists on 24 March 1794.

Coblentz (Koblenz). A German city situated at the confluence of the Moselle and Rhine rivers. In the eighteenth century, Koblenz was significant politically as the seat of the Archbishop-Elector of Trier, and so an important site in the Holy Roman Empire ruled from Vienna. After 1789, the city became a key refuge for counter-revolutionary émigrés forming an exiled court around Louis XVI's younger brothers, the comte de Provence and the comte d'Artois. The king's cousin the prince de Condé also rallied there a counter-revolutionary royalist army that took part in the ultimately unsuccessful Austrian-Prussian invasion of France in 1792. In retaliation French republican forces under général François-Séverin Marceau stormed and occupied the city in October 1794.

Cocyte (Cocytus). In Greek mythology, the Cocytus flows into the Acheron and is one of the five rivers encircling the underworld, the realm of the dead ruled by Hades.

Collot d'Herbois, Jean-Marie. A widely travelled actor and minor dramatist before 1789, Collot d'Herbois returned to Paris at the outbreak of the Revolution. In 1791, he was still an eloquent defender of the constitutional monarchy until this political position was discredited by the king's failed attempt to flee Paris in June 1791. His revolutionary fame was established with his championing of the Swiss soldiers who had mutinied against their superiors in Nancy in August 1790 (see Suisses de Châteauvieux). He secured their amnesty in December 1791 and led festivities in their honour in April 1792. It is in this role that Collot d'Herbois attracted Chénier's sustained scorn and ire, since the poet saw the fêting of the mutineers as rule by rank demagoguery and a mockery of the legal order. Collot d'Herbois's views radicalized with the Revolution. Elected to the National Convention in September 1792, he voted for the king's death in January 1793, hounded moderate republicans in the debating chamber and joined the Committee of Public Safety in the summer of that year. In the autumn of 1793 he was seconded to fight counter-revolutionary movements in the provinces, bringing the Terror to Lyon in the form of mass executions of clergy and sundry other suspects. He cleverly sided against Robespierre in the summer of 1794 but could not distance himself from his own involvement in the Terror. With his close ally, Jacques-Nicolas Billaud-Varenne, he was condemned to deportation in March 1795 and was shipped to Cayenne in French Guiana where he died of yellow fever in 1796.

Constantinople. See Byzance.

Corday, Marie-Anne-Charlotte. Corday grew up in rural Normandy and moved to Caen in 1791. A convinced republican before the Revolution due to reading Plutarch and Rousseau as an adolescent, she sympathized with the federalist republicans known as the Girondins and, like them, blamed the radical journalist Jean-Paul Marat for the massacres in the Parisian prisons in September 1792. When the Girondin *députés* were outlawed in June 1793, many fled to Caen to try and raise the region against Paris. Corday heard them speak, specifically denouncing Marat, and so she formed a secret plan to assassinate him. She travelled to Paris on 9 July and, at the second attempt, she gained entrance to Marat's apartment on the evening of 13 July. She claimed to have news of counter-revolutionary plots in Caen and was shown into Marat's study where he was working in a bath for relief of a chronic skin condition. There she stabbed him once fatally in the chest and was immediately apprehended. She was tried on 16 July and guillotined the following evening in front of a large crowd whom she awed with her composure. Charlotte Corday was a fifth-generation descendant of the great seventeenth-century playwright Pierre Corneille and she cited him in her last letter to her father written from prison. Although he did not share her republicanism, Chénier loathed Marat and admired the young woman's singlemindedness and unfailing courage, imbuing his ode to her with something of Corneille's own idealization of tragic, self-sacrificing heroism.

D

Danton, Georges-Jacques. A lawyer, originally from north-eastern France, Danton was initially active in local city politics in the Revolution. From 1791 onwards, he was a major force at the Jacobin and Cordelier Clubs and a leader in the insurrection that overthrew the monarchy on 9–10 August 1792 as well as the dominant voice in mobilizing national conscription against the invading Austrians and Prussians. However, his political enemies accused him, as Minister of Justice, of condoning, even encouraging, the prison massacres in early September 1792. Elected to the National Convention, Danton voted for Louis XVI's death. He was also instrumental in setting up both the Revolutionary Tribunal and the Committee of Public Safety in spring 1793. He was a member of the latter body until July 1793 but refused to rejoin the Committee at the start of the Terror in the autumn of the same year. As the French war effort started to prevail in December 1793, Danton called increasingly for an end to the Terror and peace with France's enemies. As a result, those looking to prolong the Terror accused him of taking bribes, abusing public funds and selling out to the enemies of the Republic. He was arrested on 30 March 1794 on the orders of the Committee of Public Safety and the Committee of General Security. A show-trial followed which ultimately condemned Danton and fourteen political allies to the guillotine on 5 April 1794.

David, Jacques-Louis. The pre-eminent artist of his generation, David's neo-classical artworks were much admired by the revolutionaries who shared their promotion of the classical values of public virtue, austerity and grandeur. David was a personal friend of Chénier in the 1780s and the poet dedicated a laudatory ode in 1791 to David's pen-and-ink drawing of the Tennis Court Oath (the improvised event that had instituted the first National Assembly in June 1789). Chénier was still professing admiration for David's art as late as March 1792, that is, long after the poet and artist had parted ways politically (see the Biography of André Chénier). David became a friend and close ally of Robespierre and was the principal organizer of the majority of large-scale revolutionary festivities from 1791 to 1794, even designing republican costumes for revolutionary officials. He was a member of the Jacobin Club and a *député* in the National Convention where he voted for the king's death. The diametrically opposed reactions to Marat's murder in July 1793 — David painting Marat as a martyr, Chénier eulogizing his assassin — help to explain why the poet refers to David in later poems with extreme contempt as well as with a hint of self-reproach for his earlier admiration of the artist. During the Terror David sat on the internal police commission, the Committee of General Security, and fully endorsed its zealous prosecution of Terrorist politics. He was fortuitously absent through illness from the session of the Convention which toppled Robespierre, although he was arrested and imprisoned as the latter's political ally from August to December 1794 and again from May to August 1795. On his release from prison David shifted political allegiance, reflected in the more conciliatory subjects of his brilliant neo-classical artworks of the late 1790s. He rallied wholeheartedly to Bonaparte's regime, becoming its chief propagandist. David was exiled by the returning Bourbon royal family in 1814 and died in Brussels in 1825.

Désilles, André. An officer of the royal infantry who tried in vain to intervene during the mutiny of Swiss soldiers at the garrison in Nancy on 30 August 1790. Stepping bravely between the mutineers and opposing royalist forces, Désilles was shot three times in the leg and died of blood poisoning a month and a half later. Initially, he was commemorated as the selfless hero of the so-called 'Nancy affair'. For many constitutional monarchists, including Chénier, he remained the victim of a violent and illegal insurrection and figures as such in their counter-narratives to the Jacobins' glorification of the Swiss mutineers in 1792.

Dumas, René-François. A judge of the Revolutionary Tribunal, recognizable by his shock of red hair, Dumas instituted the local Jacobin branch in Lons-le-Saunier in the Jura in 1790. He travelled to Paris in June 1793 in order to denounce counter-revolutionary uprisings in his region. By August 1793, he had been nominated as a deputy judge (*vice-président*) of the Revolutionary Tribunal and became its principal judge (*président*) in April 1794. For Chénier, Dumas was one of the vile cogs of the merciless judicial machine of the Terror, working in tandem with its high-profile public prosecutor, Antoine-Quentin Fouquier-Tinville. As a close ally of Robespierre, Dumas was condemned and guillotined with him on 28 July 1794.

Duport-Dutertre, Marguerite-Louis-François. A Parisian lawyer who became Minister for Justice in November 1790, he was relieved of his post in March 1792 for resisting calls for war. After the fall of the monarchy in August 1792, Duport-Dutertre was indicted along with Antoine Barnave and other former constitutional monarchists. He was tried and guillotined with Barnave in late November 1793. Chénier cites him along with Barnave and Le Chapelier as intelligent, moderate victims of revolutionary extremism. Unwittingly or not, Chénier may have confused him in his mind with Adrien Duport who was also a moderate constitutionalist, ally of Barnave, and founding member of the Feuillant Club. Adrien Duport was also arrested in August 1792. However, when he was granted provisional release, this Duport prudently fled France for Switzerland and died there in 1798.

E

Égée (Aegean). A sea formed between the Greek and Turkish peninsulas as part of the eastern Mediterranean. It contains a number of islands famous in Antiquity.

Élide (Elis). A region of ancient Greece situated in the western Peloponnese. Its main river is the Alpheus (Alfeiós) which runs past the sacred site of Olympus where the first Olympic games were held in the eighth century BCE. Another river crossing the region, the Peneus (Pineiós), is associated with the god of love Eros.

Élysée (Elysium). Also known as the Champs Élysées or Elysian Fields, according to certain ancient Greek cults, this is a blessed place in the underworld reserved for the afterlife of heroes, those chosen by the gods, the virtuous and the just.

Eschyle (Aeschylus). Fifth-century BCE Greek playwright, regarded as the father of tragedy. Chénier refers to Aeschylus's *The Persians*, a dramatic representation of the Greek victory over the Persians in the second Persian invasion of Greece in 480–79 BCE. The playwright had personally participated in the battle of Marathon (490 BCE) which had ended the first Persian invasion. Aeschylus thus stands as both an ethical and aesthetic antithesis to the mediocre Jacobins celebrating the liberation of forty Swiss mutineers in 1792 (see Suisses de Châteauvieux).

Euclide (Euclid). Greek mathematician from Alexandria active during the reign of Ptolemy I (323–283 BCE). He is mentioned by Chénier since Euclidean geometry, set out in the foundational textbook *The Elements*, was central to calculations in astronomy.

Eudoxe (Eudoxus). A fourth-century BCE mathematician and astronomer from Cnidus in Asia Minor (today Turkey). He is most famous for a pioneering geometrical theory of planetary movements that influenced Euclid.

F

Fanny (Françoise Lecouteulx). Françoise-Charlotte Lecouteulx de la Noraye was the daughter of the eminent banker Louis Pourrat and his wife Madeleine. She married Laurent-Vincent Lecouteulx before the Revolution and in 1787 they bought the elegant Château de Voisins in Louveciennes to the north of Versailles. The Lecouteulx were an influential banking family (her brother-in-law would survive the Terror to become one of the founders of the Banque de France in 1800) and held progressive social views. Along with famous writers and *philosophes* like Laclos and Condorcet, Chénier was a regular guest at Voisins, especially from 1791 onwards as the family's moderate constitutional monarchism was overtaken by revolutionary events and they sought to distance themselves from the political radicalism of the capital. In April 1793, Chénier sought refuge in Versailles and often crossed the royal parks to Louveciennes in order to visit Mme Pourrat and her two daughters, Françoise, and Jeanne-Jacqueline, wife of the marquis Hocquart de Turtot. It was in the course of these visits that Chénier seems to have fallen deeply and secretly in love with Françoise whom he nicknames Fanny in a series of lyrical *Odes à Fanny* composed over the spring and early summer of 1793. He also wrote the moving 'Sur la mort d'un enfant' in the summer of 1793 in commemoration of the loss of Françoise's first daughter in February 1792. The mother and her other daughter were also in declining health and would only survive the Terror by seventeen months or so. In August 1793, Louis Pourrat and Laurent Lecouteulx were placed under house arrest. As prominent bankers, they were highly suspect to the authorities of the Terror and were imprisoned as foreign agents on 3 December 1793. Pourrat was executed on 9 July 1794 in the company of Marie-Antoinette's favourite architect Richard Mique, sixteen days before Chénier himself went to the guillotine.

Fouquier-Tinville, Antoine-Quentin. A lawyer from northern France who served as a prosecutor in the Châtelet courts in Paris before the Revolution, he came to prominence after the fall of the monarchy in August 1792; and in March 1793, at the institution of the Revolutionary Tribunal, he was appointed as its public prosecutor in chief. Through the Terror his prosecutions increasingly bore only a veneer of legality and were marked by ruthless ideological conviction for the extremist politics of the time. As such, he was despised by Chénier as one of the most sinister instruments of the Terror — long before he added fabricated accusations to the charge-sheet drawn up on 20 July 1794 against the poet and his fellow accused. Fouquier-Tinville survived the fall of Robespierre only long enough to prosecute his former political master and his associates and see them guillotined. He was arrested on 1 August 1794 and claimed at his trial that he had merely obeyed the orders of the Committee of Public Safety. His defence was not credible and he was eventually executed on 7 May 1795 along with fifteen other former functionaries of the Revolutionary Tribunal. He appears as a character in Umberto Giordano's *verismo* opera *Andrea Chénier* (1896).

G

Garat, Dominique-Joseph. Born in Bayonne in the semi-autonomous French Basque country, Garat was an established writer before the Revolution, contributing notably to the progressive *Encyclopédie méthodique* and the widely read gazette the *Mercure de France*. Elected to the Estates-General in 1789, he also wrote for the *Journal de Paris*. Garat was appointed Minister of Justice in late 1792 and was thus charged with communicating the death sentence to Louis XVI. In January 1793 he became Minister for the Interior and it is in this guise that Chénier cites him mockingly as 'le bon Garat', as a minister known for a degree of personal integrity that sat ill with his condoning the political intimidation, corruption and excesses of those around Marat and the Jacobins. Garat resigned from his post on 20 August 1793 and was arrested in early October of the same year for alleged political sympathy with the outlawed federalist Girondins. He was released shortly afterwards and was protected during the Terror because of his former friendship with Robespierre. He nonetheless took sides against Robespierre in July 1794 and went on to serve subsequent political regimes until 1809, emerging at the same time as a vocal defender of Basque particularism. Garat died in 1833 and left interesting memoirs and a study of the origins of the Basque people.

Grouvelle, Philippe-Antoine. Before the Revolution Grouvelle was for a time secretary to the king's cousin the prince de Condé and wrote an operetta that was performed at Versailles. He was a member of the moderate Société de 1789, as was Chénier, and contributed frequently to the popular educational weekly *La Feuille villageoise*. At the overthrow of the monarchy in August 1792, Grouvelle became secretary to the new revolutionary executive council and, with Garat, he had a hand in communicating the news of the death sentence to Louis XVI in January 1793. In May 1793 he was appointed as French representative to the kingdom of Denmark, remaining in this post until 1800. He died in 1806. Grouvelle is mentioned contemptuously by Chénier because of his political trajectory from fellow moderate constitutional monarchist to republican functionary active in handing down the king's death sentence.

H

Harmodius. In concert with his lover Aristogeiton, Harmodius assassinated the Athenian tyrant Hipparchus in 514 BCE. Hipparchus ruled with his brother Hippias who survived the assassination attempt. After stabbing Hipparchus to death, Harmodius was struck down on the spot by a guardsman while Aristogeiton was arrested, tortured then executed by Hippias. Ruling alone, Hippias enforced a still more ferocious tyranny until he was overthrown by the Athenians, aided by a Spartan army, in 508 BCE. The subsequent Athenian democracy raised a statue to Harmodius and Aristogeiton as the so-called Tyrannicides. Chénier obviously holds up 'Harmodius alongside his friend' as noble classical models vindicating Charlotte Corday's assassination of the 'tyrant' Marat, even though Corday was adamant that she acted on her own.

Heracles. Better known by his Roman name of Hercules, Heracles was a demi-god, born of Zeus and the mortal Alcmene, thereby incurring the enduring enmity of Zeus's goddess-queen Hera. He was the greatest of all ancient Greek heroes, a paragon of masculinity and redresser of innumerable wrongs (and as such taken as a revolutionary republican idol in 1793). Heracles undertook and completed twelve superhuman 'labours' in expiation for the crime of having murdered his own children when he had been driven temporarily mad by Hera. He was also numbered among Jason's Argonauts (see Argonautes). The highly elliptical reference to Heracles as Alcide in Chénier's ode 'O mon esprit, au sein des cieux', seems to relate to the demi-god diverting the two rivers of the Elis region, the Alpheus and the Peneus, in order to wash clean the Augean stables in the fifth of his labours.

Hermès (Hermes). The son of Zeus, messenger of the gods, and the particular deity of heralds, orators, travellers, merchants and thieves. Hermes was thought to travel freely between divine and mortal worlds. A parallel Egyptian tradition, syncretized with the ancient Greek one, holds Hermes to be 'Trismegistus' or thrice-great, since he is at once a supreme philosopher, priest and king able to sound the deepest mysteries of nature, religion and politics. As such, he was credited with composing the alphabet, inventing astronomy and the law, as well as devising musical scales and weights and measures. It is this latter tradition that Chénier refers to when he chose the name of Hermes as the title for a projected 10,000-line epic philosophical poem relating the cosmogony of the Earth and the evolution of western civilization from Antiquity to the present. However, only a few draft fragments, marked with the triangular Δ sign, are extant, dating from between *c.* 1782 and 1792.

Hipparque (Hipparchus). A second-century BCE Greek mathematician and geographer, Hipparchus is considered one of the greatest ancient astronomers. He was among the first to compile a catalogue of the stars and to model accurately the motions of the sun and moon.

Hippolyte (Hippolytus). Son of Theseus, the mythical founder and king of Athens, and Hippolyta, queen of the Amazons. Hippolytus rejected the advances of his step-mother, Theseus's second wife, Phaedra. Enraged by the rejection, Phaedra told Theseus that his son had raped her. Theseus then cursed Hippolytus with one of three wishes granted to him by the sea-god Poseidon. A sea-monster thus arose to terrorize Hippolytus's horses who dragged him to his death. The story was especially well-known in France through Jean Racine's tragedy *Phèdre* (1677). Chénier's reference to the myth in his incomplete verse 'J'ai lu qu'un batelier' is comic and bathetic, suggesting that the rash and foolish revolutionaries seizing the reins of power would similarly lose control and be dashed to death in the end.

J

Jacobins, Les. A political club initially created for the *députés* to the first National Assembly and officially called the 'Société des amis de la Constitution', it was better known as the Jacobin Club because from October 1789 it met in the refectory of the so-called Couvent des Jacobins, a disaffected Dominican monastery on the rue Saint-Honoré. It grew in both membership and radical influence from 1790 to 1794. The club opened its membership to *non-députés*, including foreigners, from January 1790 and established a network of affiliated clubs in the provinces, numbering more than 150 by August 1790. This model of a centralized network was reinforced in 1790 by the creation of a correspondence committee and the club's own news-letter or journal. It opened its meetings to the public in October 1791. By this time the club's initial progressive but moderate political stance had been radicalized by events. The founding membership was severely split over Louis XVI's attempted flight from Paris in June 1791, resulting in the majority of conservative members leaving to form the pro-monarchist Feuillant Club and the small 'rump' left to advocate a more aggressive republican programme. Over 1791–92 the Jacobins were dominated by the federalist republicans of the Gironde who pushed France into war with Austria and Prussia. However, with the overthrow of the monarchy in August 1792, the dominant voices became those around the Paris-based *députés* Danton, Robespierre and Marat, arguing for the king's execution and for heavily centralized, interventionist republican government. The Jacobins both within government and outside it reached the height of their power in 1793, with key members on the executive Committee of Public Safety and an estimated 6,000 affiliated clubs throughout the country drawing on a membership of more than 500,000. 1794 saw murderous infighting between factions in the Jacobins and the Convention grouped around Robespierre, the theorist of the Terror, the extremist demagogue Hébert, and the more moderate Danton who sought an end to both the Terror and the war. This ultimately resulted in the downfall of all three groups and the closure of the Jacobin Club on 27 July 1794. The club was officially dissolved on 12 November 1794. As early as August 1790, Chénier had been one of the first journalists to denounce the Jacobins' populist, centralizing, republican tendencies. This enmity hardened over the Jacobins' championing of the Swiss mutineers in April 1792 (see Suisses de Châteauvieux), their decisive support for the king's execution in January 1793 and their role in fomenting the subsequent civil war and Terror.

Jourdan, Mathieu-Jouve. A former butcher, farrier, soldier and thief, Jourdan was an innkeeper in Paris at the outbreak of the Revolution. A vocal and violent figure in the crowds storming the Bastille in July 1789 and Versailles in October 1789, he boasted that he had personally decapitated the governor of the Bastille, the marquis de Launay, earning himself the nickname of 'Coupe-tête'. He moved to Avignon in 1790 where he agitated against the local papal authorities and participated in their overthrow in June 1790 and in the subsequent annexation of this papal enclave by the French state in August-September 1791. Following popular unrest between citizens still loyal to the Church and anti-clerical revolutionaries, Jourdan, as commander of the fort in the Papal Palace, avenged the death of a local revolutionary official by overseeing the massacre of sixty locals rounded up in the so-called Tour de la Glacière in the Palace prisons on the night of 16–17 October 1791. He was due to be brought to justice for this mass-murder but was released on the general amnesty ordered by the National Assembly in March 1792. He returned to Avignon and took up the post of commander of the Vaucluse gendarmerie. However, further barbaric excesses in this role led to his arrest in April 1794, extradition to Paris, rapid judgement and summary guillotining on 27 May 1794. For Chénier, Jourdan is the archetypal revolutionary thug employed and empowered by the Jacobin-led regime.

K

King Mob. In June 1780 huge crowds in London protested against relaxing the laws on anti-Catholic discrimination. They were led by Lord George Gordon, head of the Protestant Association. The protests degenerated into violence, with widespread rioting and looting, commonly known now as the Gordon Riots. Catholic churches, foreign embassies, the Bank of England and Newgate Prison were all attacked. At Newgate prison, a large number of inmates were freed and the building was gutted. In graffiti on the prison walls, the attackers claimed that they were authorized in their actions by 'His Majesty King Mob'.

L

Laclos, Pierre-Ambroise-François Choderlos de. An artillery officer made famous before the Revolution by his brilliant epistolary novel, *Les Liaisons dangereuses* (1782). In 1788, Laclos left the army and entered the service of the king's liberal cousin, Louis-Philippe duc d'Orléans. From 1789 to 1791, Laclos was seen as the scheming genius behind the increasingly overt plans to depose Louis XVI and replace him with a regency headed by the duc d'Orléans, especially in the wake of the king's failed escape attempt in June 1791. Laclos was also active in the Jacobin Club, founding and editing the club's journal in October 1790. As republicanism gained ground, Laclos grew more distant from his former political master and re-entered military service, contributing to the initial republican victories of autumn 1792. However, his so-called

'Orléaniste' past caught up with him in April 1793 after the duc's son deserted with General Dumouriez and passed over to the Austrians, leading to the arrest and imprisonment of Orléans, now calling himself 'Philippe Égalité'. Laclos was arrested on 5 November 1793. The following day the former duc d'Orléans was guillotined and Laclos was incarcerated first at La Force prison and then at Picpus. He nonetheless survived the Terror and was finally freed on 1 December 1794. His attempts to rejoin the army were frustrated until Bonaparte made him an artillery general in 1800. Laclos died in service at Taranto in southern Italy in September 1803. He would be personally known to Chénier through the former's relations with the Pourrat family (see Fanny). The poet cites Laclos dismissively in his 'Voûtes du Panthéon', not because the novelist was particularly close to Marat politically; the slighting reference is more likely based on Laclos's sulphurous reputation as an arch-intriguer for Orleanism and his former role as editor of the Jacobin journal.

Lacroix, Jean-François de. A lawyer from the Eure-et-Loir region, Lacroix (also known as Delacroix) was elected to the National Assembly in October 1791. He befriended Danton and was vociferous in his anti-monarchism and anti-clericalism. He joined the Committee of Public Safety at its inception in April 1793 but left it with Danton in July of the same year. From as early as 1791, rumours circulated about his corruption and fraudulent appropriation and misuse of public funds. Lacroix was caught in the general denunciation, arrest and imprisonment of the so-called Dantonists and went to the guillotine with them on 5 April 1794. For Chénier, he was the epitome of the corrupt, loudmouth political lackeys supporting the Jacobins.

Lafayette, Gilbert du Motier, marquis de. Famous before 1789 for his service under Washington in the American War of Independence, Lafayette was a leading light of the early Revolution, appointed as commander-in-chief of the newly formed National Guard in July 1789. In this role, he swore allegiance to the revolutionary regime in front of delegations of his national militia and a crowd of some 300,000 at the Fête de la Fédération in July 1790. A year later, however, when the radical clubs in Paris sought to depose Louis XVI after his failed escape attempt in June 1791, Lafayette ordered his troops to fire on the crowds in the so-called Champ-de-Mars Massacre of 17 July 1791. From this point onwards, his popularity waned and he adopted an ever more conservative political stance in the face of widespread radicalization. Lafayette resigned from the National Guard in October 1791 and was roundly beaten in his bid to be elected mayor of Paris a month later. When war on Austria was declared in April 1792, he took command of citizens' army units but found them ill-prepared and mutinous. He blamed the radical clubs in Paris and openly attacked them before the National Assembly in late June 1792. His fate was clearly tied to that of the beleaguered monarchy that was overthrown on 10 August 1792. A warrant was issued for Lafayette's arrest four days later. He deserted his army post, hoping to travel to the United States, but was taken prisoner in the Austrian Netherlands (today Belgium). Lafayette remained a prisoner of war, held in various central

European gaols, for the following five years. He and his family only returned to France in 1800 when Bonaparte restored his French citizenship. He returned to politics under the Bourbon Restoration as a liberal in the Chamber of Deputies from 1815 to 1823. At the age of 72, he was reappointed commander of the National Guard in the July Revolution of 1830. He died in 1834. Chénier generally subscribed to Lafayette's political line as a centre-ground constitutional monarchist and voted for him in the November 1791 mayoral elections in Paris.

Le Chapelier, Isaac-René-Guy. A Breton lawyer elected to the Estates-General in 1789, Le Chapelier was president of the new National Assembly in August of that year and thus presided over the abolition of 'feudalism'. He also lent his name to a liberal law banning guilds, corporations and trade unions in order to prevent workers' collectives from forming separate interests-groups in the revolutionary state. Although an early member of the Jacobin Club in late 1789, Le Chapelier came to oppose its radicalization and joined the moderate Feuillants over the summer of 1791. For the same reasons, he hastened the adoption of the monarchist constitution in September 1791. During the Terror, he temporarily emigrated to England but returned in order to oppose the confiscation of his assets. Arrested and tried summarily, he was guillotined on 22 April 1794. Chénier was sympathetic to Le Chapelier's liberalism and constitutional monarchism, and in his poem 'J'ai lu qu'un batelier' the poet associates him with other like-minded former Feuillants who fell victim to the Terror.

Le Peletier, Louis-Michel, marquis de Saint-Fargeau. A lawyer working in the Châtelet courts before the Revolution, Le Peletier was elected to the Estates-General as a representative of the nobility. However, his politics became more radical as the Revolution progressed. He presented projects in the National Assembly for the abolition of the death penalty in 1790 and fundamental educational reform in 1791 (supported in both motions by Robespierre). He was elected to the National Convention in September 1792 and sided with the Jacobins in voting for Louis XVI's death. On the eve of the king's execution, 20 January 1793, Le Peletier was stabbed to death in a restaurant in the Palais-Royal by a former royal bodyguard. The Convention honoured him with a magnificent state funeral choreographed by Jacques-Louis David. He was proclaimed a revolutionary martyr and his body was laid to rest in the Panthéon. Chénier thus presents Le Peletier's stage-managed 'martyrdom' as the template for the yet more ostentatious outpourings of grief occasioned by Marat's murder just over six months later.

Legendre, Louis. A master butcher in Paris before the Revolution, Legendre took part in the storming of the Bastille in July 1789. He was a Jacobin and a member of the popular Cordelier Club. Elected as a *député* to the National Convention in September 1792, he was close to Marat and voted for the death of the king. He served for a while on the police body, the Committee of General Security, but left it before the Terror began. He was associated with Danton, but when the latter was indicted, Legendre distanced himself from his former ally in order to avoid trial and execution in April 1794. He laid low politically until falling in with the parliamentarians who toppled Robespierre in July 1794. He later served as a representative under the Directory. He died in 1797. Chénier mocks Legendre not only as a Jacobin and as the political ally of Marat, but because he was renowned for peppering his blustering speeches in the Convention with misquotations from the classics.

Leo. A constellation in the northern hemisphere and sign of the zodiac. It is named after the Nemean lion killed by Heracles in the first of his labours (see Heracles).

Loire, La. The longest river in France, rising in the Massif Central, running west through Nevers, Orléans, Tours and Nantes before flowing into the Atlantic Ocean. From November 1793 to January 1794, the revolutionary *député* and administrator Jean-Baptiste Carrier oversaw the mass drownings of between 1,800 and 4,000 suspected counter-revolutionaries of all ages and both sexes in the lower reaches of the Loire, just downstream from the Île de Nantes.

Louis XVI. King of France, 1774–92. A progressive, if indecisive king, Louis XVI attempted to reconcile the monarchy to the Revolution, swearing public allegiance to the new regime at the Fête de la Fédération in July 1790. However, increasingly intrusive restrictions placed on him and his family, in line with increasing religious and social tensions, led him to attempt an ill-fated escape from Paris in June 1791. This effectively discredited his rule as well as the new constitution that was hurriedly promulgated to frame it in law. Brought to the National Assembly in April 1792, Louis XVI declared war on Austria on behalf of his government. But as the French war effort rapidly unravelled, he was overthrown by popular republican forces in August 1792. He was then put on trial by the National Convention between December 1792 and January 1793. Found guilty of treason, he was sentenced to death by the slimmest of margins and guillotined on 21 January 1793. Chénier, who seems less concerned with the personal shortcomings of the king, supported a reformed, liberal monarchy set within the framework of rights granted by the first revolutionary constitution. As a result, he readily offered to help the monarchist ministry thwart the republican uprising on 10 August 1792 and put his skills as both polemicist and journalist in the service of the counsel for defence during the king's trial. He never forgave those politicians, including his younger brother, who condemned Louis XVI to death.

Lucienne (also Luciennes). The former place name for the village of Louveciennes north of Versailles (see Fanny). It is situated on a small hill that overlooks the Seine.

Lycambe (Lycambes). According to an ancient Greek tradition, Lycambes lived on the island of Paros in the seventh century BCE. He promised his daughter in marriage to the poet Archilochus only to renege on his promise shortly thereafter. This so enraged the poet that he attacked father and daughter in vicious iambic verse, driving them both to hang themselves. Chénier refers to this tradition not only to invest his own iambics with the same lethal power, but also to state that, unlike Archilochus, his cause is not personal revenge but public justice.

M

Marat, Jean-Paul. A physician and scientist before the Revolution, Marat lived in England for many years and published there his first political essay *The Chains of Slavery* (1774; French trans. 1792). He returned to France in 1776, practised as a doctor and wrote treatises on fire, electricity and light that brought him into conflict with the scientific establishment. Enthused by the outbreak of the Revolution, he threw himself into the fray as a journalist, launching his famous newspaper *L'Ami du peuple* in September 1789. He made scathing, often libellous, attacks on leading revolutionary institutions and figures, forcing him on occasion into hiding, including in the Parisian sewers, which aggravated his debilitating skin condition. As early as July 1790, he called for 300 to 600 heads to roll in order to ensure revolutionary peace and prosperity. Active in the overthrow of the monarchy in August 1792, Marat is often accused of having openly incited the Parisian prison massacres of the following month in which more than a thousand inmates were summarily executed. He was elected to the National Convention and voted for the death of the king. He then turned his rhetorical violence on the moderate republicans, known as the Girondins. In April 1793, they called for Marat's arrest and trial on charges of undermining the Convention and inciting murder. He was triumphantly acquitted by the Revolutionary Tribunal and conspired in the purge of the Girondins from the Convention on 2 June 1793. As his skin condition worsened, he took to working from home in a medicinal bath. It was here that Charlotte Corday, a Girondin sympathizer from Caen, stabbed him to death on 13 July 1793. Marat's assassination led to his revolutionary apotheosis: Jacques-Louis David organized his state funeral and painted him as an iconic revolutionary martyr. He was initially buried in the garden of the radical Cordeliers Club to which he belonged, and in the Terror his bust often replaced that of saints in desacralized churches. Calls soon came for the transfer of his remains to the Panthéon, including one made to the Convention by Chénier's younger brother, Marie-Joseph, in November 1793. Marat's remains were eventually pantheonized on 12 September 1794 but by this time the political tide had turned in reaction to the Terror, and a more conservative regime saw to it that his coffin was removed from the Panthéon in February 1795 and his busts were widely smashed. Chénier despised Marat in his lifetime as a violent demagogue; but he despised even more the hagiographic cult than grew up around him in death, writing some of his most withering iambics on Marat's 'martyrdom' and the calls to transfer his remains to the Panthéon.

Mars. The Roman god of war, identified with the Greek god Ares, although the Greek god was often regarded more harshly as a destructive, destabilizing force. Mars was the god of the conquering Roman armies and his cult spread across the empire. Chénier mentions Mars in his great Pindaric ode 'O mon esprit, au sein des cieux'. This was most probably written in December 1793, and formed part of a troubled response to the triumphant contemporary reports of French military victories over the armies of the First Coalition of European monarchies.

Ménades, Les (Maenads). In Greek mythology, the maenads were the female followers of the god of wine and fecundity, Dionysus. They are often portrayed, intoxicated and dancing, in states of ecstatic frenzy. Their ecstasy could also turn murderous, as in their tearing to pieces of the poet-musician Orpheus, deemed to have profaned the temple of Dionysus. Chénier refers to the maenads in his 'Fragment: Un vulgaire assassin va chercher les ténèbres', in which the classical name is given derisively to violent Parisian women of the lowest social orders who marched on Versailles in October 1789. The women allegedly incited the murder of a number of royal guards at the palace before parading their heads on pikes as part of the carnivalesque escort accompanying the royal family back to Paris. The image was a common one at the time, found notably in Edmund Burke's *Reflections on the Revolution in France* (1790).

Mirabeau, Honoré-Gabriel Riqueti, comte de. Acquiring a scandalous reputation before the Revolution as a womanizer, gambler and hack writer, Mirabeau travelled in the Dutch Republic and England in the 1780s. He honed his oratorical style in a series of subsequent political pamphlets against hereditary nobility, financial speculation and royal corruption. Elected to the Estates-General as a representative of the Third Estate, or commoners, despite his nobility, Mirabeau emerged as the leading orator of the early Revolution, 1789–90. He advocated a British-style constitutional monarchy, based on a strong ministry enacting laws established in the National Assembly as a settlement between the king and his people. As the Revolution diverged increasingly from this political vision, Mirabeau became a secret adviser to the royal court, with the Crown using Austrian money to pay off his personal debts. At the same time Mirabeau was a leading light in the Jacobin Club from its inception in October 1789, becoming its president in December 1790. Politically highly astute, Mirabeau was nonetheless stymied in his ambitions by increasing revolutionary radicalism and by the monarchy's reluctance to take a stand against it. Suffering from heart trouble from early 1791 onwards, and despite the attentions of his personal doctor Cabanis, Mirabeau died on 2 April 1791. He was widely and sincerely mourned and the Panthéon was instituted to receive his remains later in the same month, as its first 'grand homme'. However, after the overthrow of the monarchy, the discovery in November 1792 of Mirabeau's secret correspondence with the king and queen led to his posthumous disgrace. His bust was smashed in the Jacobin Club and his body was eventually disinterred from the Panthéon to be replaced by that of Marat in September 1794. Chénier, whose constitutional monarchism was largely in line with Mirabeau's, cites him approvingly in April 1792, pitting Mirabeau's statesmanlike defence of the legal order against the clamorous populism of the Jacobins in their support of the Swiss mutineers of Nancy (see Suisses de Châteauvieux).

Moniteur, Le. Founded in November 1789, *La Gazette nationale ou Le Moniteur universel* was a highly influential newspaper during the Revolution largely because it offered reports and transcriptions of key debates in the National Assembly, with little or no comment, making it a relatively objective record of the dominant ideology of the moment. It became the official organ of Bonaparte's regime shortly after his *coup d'état* in November 1799. Chénier mentions the newspaper in his iambics 'On dit que le dédain froid et silencieux' as the source of a bombastic speech made by Barère on 28 January 1794 about the populist reform of French diction.

Montagne, La (The Mountain). A radical political grouping sitting on the highest benches on the left of the National Convention, hence the name. Its *députés* were collectively referred to as 'Montagnards' or 'Mountain Men'. They first coalesced in favour of regicide during the king's trial in January 1793. This pitted them, with increasing hostility, against the more moderate republicans, known as the Girondins. This factional opposition was exacerbated by geographical factors, since the Girondins largely represented provincial France while the Montagnards had their political power base in Paris and responded to shifts in popular opinion in the capital. Outside the Convention, they drew membership from both Jacobin and Cordelier Clubs. The *députés* of The Mountain succeeded in evicting the Girondins from the Convention in June 1793 and swiftly drafted a new radical constitution for the revolutionary regime which was approved by plebiscite in August 1793. However, this so-called Montagnard Constitution was suspended at the outbreak of the Terror and never implemented thereafter. The Montagnards nonetheless dictated revolutionary policy through their heavy presence on the Committee of Public Safety. The Mountain fell to internal factionalism in 1794 and effectively ended with the arrest and execution of Robespierre and his associates in July of that year. Chénier refers to The Mountain as a set of violent and corrupt demagogues willing to take up Marat's mantle after his murder in July 1793.

Muses, Les (Muses). In Greek mythology, the Muses were the inspirational goddesses of the arts, literature and sciences. The daughters of Zeus and the Titan goddess of memory, Mnemosyne, they are traditionally nine in number. Chénier imagines them outraged at the uncultured revolutionary jargonizing heard in the Convention, covering Barère in particular with opprobrium and insult.

N

Nantes. Important city on the Loire river, capital of the *département* of Loire-Atlantique. Before the Revolution, Nantes was the largest port in France responsible for almost half of the French Atlantic slave trade and the import of its principal products (sugar, rum, coffee, cotton, tobacco, cacao, indigo dye). Initially supportive of the Revolution, the city became a centre of royalist and Catholic counter-revolution as part of the more general Vendée uprising in 1793. Hence a large republican garrison was stationed there and

Jean-Baptiste Carrier was sent from Paris to organize the suppression of all suspected counter-revolutionaries. When the city centre was ravaged with famine and a typhus epidemic, the revolutionary authorities transferred the city's prisoners to the huge coffee warehouse, the Entrepôt des Cafés, on the northern bank of the Loire opposite the Île de Nantes. By December 1793 the prison was overpopulated with between 8,000 and 9,000 inmates. From here a military commission organized the mass-shooting of counter-revolutionaries in the Gigant quarry and Carrier oversaw the mass-drowning of between 1,800 and 4,000 people between November 1793 and January 1794. The prison was overrun with typhus, accounting for a further 2,000 deaths, and was so infected and noxious that it had to be closed in late January 1794.

Némésis (Nemesis). In Greek mythology, Nemesis is the goddess of divine retribution meting out justice to those who indulge in hubris, that is, arrogance before the gods. By extension, she is invoked as a belated but implacable avenger of crime and is often depicted as a winged goddess carrying a sword or dagger. For Chénier, Charlotte Corday is an instrument of Nemesis, visiting a just death sentence on the overreaching criminal, Marat.

Nymphes (Nymphs). According to ancient Greek folklore, nymphs were divine spirits animating nature and were often identified with particular rivers, seas, lakes, woods and mountains. Usually depicted as beautiful young women, they were not necessarily immortal. Nymphs feature prominently in Chénier's bucolic poetry before the Revolution and can be seen as an expression of his broader pantheism.

O

Ormuz (Ormus). A famous Persian sultanate flourishing *c.* 1100–1700 CE, situated in the Persian Gulf and centred on the fortified port of Hormuz. As it controlled sea-trade between the Middle East and Eastern Africa, India and China, it was extremely prosperous and so became a poetic image for exotic opulence.

Orphée (Orpheus). According to ancient Greek tradition, Orpheus was a legendary poet-musician and prophet. It was frequently claimed that his music could tame wild beasts and induce trees and rocks to dance. He was son of the Thracian king Oeagrus and the muse of epic poetry Calliope and, in his turn, the civilizing king, priest and legislator of Thrace. When his wife Eurydice died from a snakebite, Orpheus descended into the underworld to retrieve her, charming all whom he met with his music and singing. Hades promised to release Eurydice, provided that Orpheus did not look back as she followed him out of the underworld. However, at the very last moment, he turned around and lost her forever. Orpheus is also numbered among Jason's Argonauts and his music and knowledge of the stars helped to pilot the ship to its goal. He died in Thrace, torn apart by maenads enraged at the musician's profanation of a temple to Dionysus, their tutelary god. His severed head and lyre still sang and sounded as they floated down the river Hebrus. Chénier identified closely with Orpheus both through his Greek ancestry and as a lyric poet. However, the reference to Orpheus in his 'Hymne sur l'entrée triomphale des Suisses révoltés du régiment de Châteauvieux' is a barbed taunt at all the mediocre rhymers who celebrated the rehabilitated Swiss mutineers in April 1792, chief among whom was Chénier's younger brother, Marie-Joseph.

P

Palès (Pales). Roman deity of shepherds and flocks who was invoked as a goddess or a god or even as a pair of gods.

Panthéon, Le (Pantheon). Initially designed and constructed in the late eighteenth century as the neo-classical Catholic church of Sainte Geneviève in the Latin Quarter in Paris, the building was transformed into a national mausoleum by a decree of the National Assembly in April 1791. Its name and use were modelled on the Pantheon in Rome. The interior of the former church was darkened and its religious friezes and statues replaced through 1791 with murals on patriotic themes. Mirabeau was the first distinguished citizen to be given the honours of 'panthéonisation' in April 1791, followed three months later by the exhumed remains of Voltaire. However, the dead were not immune to the political vicissitudes of the Revolution: Mirabeau's remains were removed from the Panthéon in September 1794 to be replaced by those of Marat, whose own coffin would be thrown out four months later. From February 1795 onwards, it was decreed that no one could be placed in the Panthéon until at least ten years after his or her death.

Parnasse, Le (Mount Parnassus). A mountain in central Greece rising above Delphi, sacred to the gods Dionysus and Apollo, and home to the nine Muses. In this last respect, Parnassus is used symbolically to mean the home of poetry, music, the arts and sciences. Chénier subverts this image to contrast lofty Muse-inspired poetry with the debased, sycophantic verse produced at Marat's death by poetasters such as Michel de Cubières. 'Parnasse' might also refer to the Montparnasse quarter of Paris, which was the ironic name originally given by seventeenth-century student-poets to a gravel mound on the southern outskirts of the city and which had become a place of popular entertainments by the time of the Revolution.

Paros. A Greek island in the Aegean Sea, famous in Antiquity for its white translucent marble that was used from the sixth century BCE onwards in classical sculpture. Paros was also home to the seventh-century BCE Greek iambic poet Archilochus. It thus has a double resonance for Chénier in contrasting the classical whiteness of Paros with the bloody mire of revolutionary Paris and in furnishing him with a classical poetic model (iambics) with which to savage the Jacobin-led regime.

Persans, Les (Persians). The principal enemies of the ancient Greeks, most notably in the celebrated wars fought during the two Persian invasions of Greece in the late fifth century BCE. Chénier refers specifically to the tragic playwright Aeschylus's *The Persians* and the lyric poet Pindar's *Pythian Odes*, both of which celebrate the Greek victory in the wake of the second Persian invasion of 480–79 BCE.

Philomèle (Philomela or Philomel). In Greek mythology, Philomela was the sister of Procne, wife of the Thracian king, Tereus. Most modern accounts draw on that of Ovid, according to which Tereus raped his sister-in-law and then cut out her tongue to silence her. Philomela then wove a tapestry telling her story and sent it to her sister Procne. Together they took their revenge by murdering Tereus's son and feeding him to the king. When, at the end of the meal, the sisters presented Tereus with his son's severed head, he rose in fury to attack them. To save the sisters, the gods transformed them respectively into a nightingale (Philomela) and a swallow (Procne). The violence of the myth has led the nightingale's song to be traditionally interpreted as mournful lamentation. Hence Chénier associates Philomela's story of abuse and lament with the voice of his fellow prisoner in Saint-Lazare, Aimée de Coigny, whom he ventriloquizes through his ode 'La Jeune Captive'.

Phocide (Phocis). A central region of ancient Greece that includes Mount Parnassus and the religious centre of Delphi. Chénier mentions Phocis in relation to the myth of the young god Apollo slaying the monstrous Python there in the temple of the Delphic oracle.

Pindare (Pindar). A fifth-century BCE Greek lyric poet from Thebes, often held to be the greatest of the classical lyric poets, although his work is difficult in places due to the use of obscure periphrases and esoteric terms. He innovated in all the poetic genres he inherited, especially in the ode. Many of these rich and resounding poems were written for the victors of the games at Panhellenic festivals. His work had something of a revival in late eighteenth-century France, mainly through the imitations of Pindaric odes practised by the neo-classical poet Ponce-Denis Écouchard Lebrun, nicknamed 'Lebrun-Pindare'. Lebrun was a mentor and admirer of Chénier's work, read in manuscript, before the Revolution. Chénier cites Pindar, along with Aeschylus, for his odes in celebration of the Greek victories over the Persians in 480–79 BCE, even if these poetic tributes were not originally appreciated in Pindar's native Thebes because of the city's long-standing rivalry with Athens. In his last poems, Chénier rarely imitates the Pindaric ode itself, with the obvious exception of his declamatory 'O mon esprit, au sein des cieux', most probably written in December 1793, and which retains the formal Pindaric stanza-structure of a tripartite strophe/antistrophe/epode. It also adopts and adapts the Pindaric theme of the impassively triumphant athlete.

Plough, The. A strongly visible pattern of seven stars in the northern hemisphere, forming part of the constellation Ursa Major. Also known as the Big Dipper.

Python. A huge serpent and son of Gaia, goddess of the Earth, Python guarded his mother's sanctuary at Delphi, which was thought at the time to be the centre of the world. The monstrous serpent was killed by Apollo who thus became the tutelary deity of the shrine and the city. However, Apollo's murder of Python within the sanctuary itself was a violation that had to be expiated by the institution of a Panhellenic festival held in Delphi every four years, the so-called Pythian games.

R

Râpée, La. The name of a faubourg of Paris on the right bank of the Seine famous for its cabarets and places of popular entertainment. In April 1792, at the time of the controversial celebration of the Swiss mutineers, it was frequented by the Jacobin mayor of Paris, Jérôme Pétion, and radical members of the city council or Commune de Paris.

Robespierre, Maximilien. A lawyer from Arras, elected to the Estates-General in May 1789, Robespierre steadily imposed himself as a radical voice in the National Assembly, voting for the abolition of the death penalty, minority voting rights and sweeping educational reforms. He was a prominent member of the Jacobin Club from its inception and rose to become its dominant figure. He opposed the war with Austria and Prussia in 1792 and supported the overthrow of the monarchy in August of the same year. Elected to the National Convention, Robespierre made a number of decisive interventions in Louis XVI's trial and voted for the king's death in January 1793. He sat with the hard-line *députés* of La Montagne (see Montagne) and opposed the federalist Girondins. In the summer of 1793 he joined the Committee of Public Safety and became one of its most influential and incisive members. He not only supported the politics of the Terror, initiated in September 1793, but developed an ideology of Terror and Virtue that sought the extension of these policies on a longer-term basis. In defence of this vision of the Revolution, Robespierre and his associates ruthlessly eliminated rival factions (around Hébert and Danton) in the spring of 1794. After instituting a national deist cult of the Supreme Being and leading a festival in its honour in early June 1794, Robespierre was increasingly suspected of aspiring to a Roman-style dictatorship. A coalition of extremists and moderates thus brought him down in a parliamentary coup on 27 July 1794 and he and twenty-one close political allies were guillotined the following day. Chénier was hostile to Robespierre on the general grounds of his radical republican politics: his leading roles in the Jacobin Club, as a Montagnard *député*, and as a key member of the Committee of Public Safety during the Terror. But he also openly opposed him on specific issues, such as Robespierre's vocal support for the Swiss mutineers in April 1792 expressed in both a speech at Jacobin Club and in an article for a radical news-sheet on the day of the festival itself.

S

Seine, La. A major French river running through Paris and Rouen before flowing into the English Channel at Le Havre. The Seine runs in scenic meanders below Louveciennes downstream from Paris, where Chénier spent time in 1793 with Françoise 'Fanny' Lecouteulx and her family at the Château de Voisins.

Suisses de Châteauvieux, Les. The name of an army regiment, stationed at Nancy in August 1790 that mutinied over pay. In the ensuing unrest and violence, approximately 300 people were killed or injured, including the young lieutenant Désilles who had stepped into the firing-line to call a truce. The mutiny was eventually put down by troops loyal to the king and an extraordinary military tribunal sentenced twenty-two Swiss mutineers to death by hanging. It also sent forty-one more to the galleys for thirty years and incarcerated a further seventy-two. However, after an appeal by the Jacobin Collot d'Herbois, the National Assembly amnestied the forty-one galley slaves in December 1791. Continually and noisily championed by the Jacobins and Marat, these same mutineers were 'liberated' from their prison in Brest in late March 1792 and declared the heroes of a 'fête de la Liberté' proposed and organized in Paris by the Jacobin Club, controversially funded by public monies. Chénier reacted furiously and repeatedly in a series of articles published in the *Journal de Paris* to what he saw as an affront to the legal order and as the consecration of mob rule. Crucially, for his later poetry during the Revolution, on the day of the festival itself (15 April 1792) he chose to satirize and ridicule those involved in the festivities in the iambic verse form associated with the ancient Greek poet Archilochus. Thus, the *Journal de Paris* published the first of his iambics, the bitterly ironic 'Hymne sur l'entrée triomphale des Suisses révoltés du régiment de Châteauvieux'.

T

Thémis (Themis). In Greek mythology, Themis is a Titaness incarnating divine order, natural law and universal justice. Her symbols are the scales of justice and a sword to divide fact from fiction. Temporal or human justice, called 'Dike' by the ancient Greeks, was the daughter of Themis and Zeus, according to Hesiod. Chénier invokes the Titaness's name in his verse 'Comme un dernier rayon' as a seemingly absent or ineffectual power in the desolate world he sees about him in the Terror.

Thrace. A region in south-east Europe covering parts of present-day Bulgaria, Greece and Turkey. It is bounded by the Balkan Mountains to the north, the Aegean Sea to the south and the Black Sea to the east. In Greek mythology, Thrace was a sorceress and sister to Europa. Legendary Thracian kings include Diomedes, Tereus, Oeagrus, Orpheus and Pyreneus. The Roman poet Ovid recounts that this last king was killed pursuing the Muses whom he had sought to capture and violate. Pyreneus is then 'ce Thrace impudent' alluded to in Chénier's iambics 'On dit que le dédain froid et silencieux'.

Thuriot, Jacques-Alexis. A lawyer from Reims, Thuriot moved to Paris before the Revolution and, as a member of the municipal council in July 1789, he led an unsuccessful delegation to negotiate the surrender of the Bastille just before the fortress-prison was stormed. He was also an assiduous member of the Jacobin Club from its institution in October 1789. Elected to the Legislative Assembly in October 1791, Thuriot's politics radicalized after the declaration of war in April 1792 and he became an outspoken republican in the summer of that year, drawing close to Danton, and participating in the fall of the monarchy on 10 August 1792. He took part in the prosecution of the king's former ministers before being elected to the National Convention in September 1792. He sat with radical *députés* of La Montagne (see Montagne), voted for the death of Louis XVI and was instrumental in the purging of the moderate Girondins from the Convention in June 1793. Thuriot joined the Committee of Public Safety in July 1793 but was isolated as the only member not in favour of the politics of the Terror, resulting in his resignation from the Committee in September. He supported the more lenient political line taken by Danton, to the point of being excluded from the pro-Terror Jacobin Club in October 1793. He kept a low profile thereafter and so did not join Danton and his allies on the scaffold in April 1794. Nonetheless, the execution of his former political colleagues strengthened Thuriot's opposition to Robespierre. He thus collaborated in the latter's proscription and arrest on 27 July 1794 by using his role as the acting president of the Convention to prevent Robespierre from defending himself. As the Revolution took a more conservative turn after the fall of Robespierre, Thuriot remained largely consistent in his Jacobin beliefs. As a result, he took part in the swiftly crushed, popular uprising of 20 May 1795, having to go into hiding to avoid arrest and trial. Thuriot was appointed to senior judicial posts under Bonaparte. However, with the return of the Bourbon monarchy in 1814, he was exiled as a regicide and died in Liège, Belgium, in 1829. Chénier lists Thuriot among the more vicious and vociferous Jacobins and Montagnards in 1793, in a sense calling him out in the same way that Thuriot habitually personalized many of his own political attacks.

V

Versailles. Originally the site of a royal hunting lodge, the building was converted by Louis XIII into a château in the 1630s. In the wake of aristocratic revolts in the 1640s and early 1650s, Louis XIV sought a place of relative political autonomy distant from the volatility of the capital. He settled on Versailles, some twelve miles from the centre of Paris, and spent nearly twenty years and millions of *livres* in creating his imposing and resplendent residence there. Louis XIV made Versailles the more or less permanent seat of his court and government in 1682. Except for a brief period during Louis XV's minority at the start of the eighteenth century, it remained the principal royal residence and heart of government until 1789. After the social and political upheavals across France in the summer of 1789, harvests were disorganized and food prices soared. Rumours circulated of a famine plot organized in Versailles to starve revolutionary Paris into submission, exacerbated by stories in early October of Marie-Antoinette holding counter-revolutionary dinners for royal troops. On 5 October 1789 between 6,000 and 7,000 women from Paris marched on Versailles, followed by their menfolk and the national guard. The insurgent crowds besieged the palace and, after a tense stand-off accompanied by acts of violence killing a small number of royal guards, Louis XVI and the royal family were compelled to return to Paris escorted by jubilant crowds. With the departure of the royal family, the palace was closed. Its upkeep was entrusted to the national guard of the town of Versailles. The palace furniture and fittings were put in storage and the artworks were transferred to the Louvre in 1792. In June 1793, to help finance the war effort, the furnishings of Versailles were auctioned and the local revolutionaries of Versailles planted vegetables and fruit trees in the palace grounds. In 1795 the palace was declared a national museum. Chénier moved to 37 rue de Satory on the outskirts of the town of Versailles at the start of April 1793. Versailles was thought to be a relatively safe haven for Chénier because of its distance from the capital and because it fell within the political constituency of his younger brother, Marie-Joseph, the Jacobin deputy for the Seine-et-Oise. The poet's lodgings in Versailles looked onto the former royal vegetable plots and an artificial lake known as the Pièce d'eau des Suisses. More importantly, Chénier could walk in the nearby woods and cross the grounds of the deserted château to see Mme Pourrat and family in their Château de Voisins, near Louveciennes, some five miles to the north. He could thus be in weekly, if not daily, contact with his platonic love-interest, Françoise 'Fanny' Lecouteulx, Mme Pourrat's daughter, who was staying with her mother at the time. Chénier's ode 'A Versailles' was most likely composed in early November 1793, when its bucolic and amorous themes are interwoven with notes of creeping political fear. News had also just reached Versailles of the show-trial and serial execution of the twenty-one Girondin deputies arrested in the June of that year.

Vertu (Virtue). An ethical principle and quality in both the classical and Christian traditions. In the Revolution, it was the classical political meaning of virtue that predominated, understood as an unfailing duty to sacrifice oneself for the greater public good. This understanding drew on Montesquieu's influential *De l'esprit des lois* (1748) in which virtue is presented as the main-spring of republican government. Robespierre in particular seized on virtue as the cornerstone of a millenarian Republic of Virtue that could only be realized by the merciless elimination of all who would otherwise corrupt it, that is, those singled out for death by the politics of the Terror. The Terror was then, in his words, to be understood as an 'emanation' of virtue and its most elemental guarantee. In his iambic verse 'Comme un dernier rayon', Chénier attempts to wrest virtue from this exclusive Jacobin interpretation, suggesting that virtue is not an emanation of Terror but the self-sacrificing vocation to resist it, which the poet himself incarnates. In the same vein, Charlotte Corday's murder of Marat is presented in Chénier's ode to her as a selfless act for the greater good, the epitome of virtue in action.

Voltaire, François-Marie Arouet. Famous primarily as a poet, dramatist and historian in his lifetime, Voltaire also wrote influential philosophical tales such as *Zadig* (1748) and *Candide* (1759) where his celebrated satirical wit was given free rein. Voltaire became an increasingly vociferous advocate of freedom of religion and freedom of speech, defending the use of reason and toleration in his *Traité sur la tolérance* (1763). He died in May 1778 after making a triumphant return to Paris. Yet because of his withering attacks on the fanaticism and hypocrisy of the Catholic Church, friends and admirers deemed it wise to smuggle his body out of Paris to be buried secretly at the Abbaye de Scellières, a dependence of Voltaire's nephew, some seventy-five miles to the east of the capital. Although no supporter of democracy, Voltaire was idolized by the revolutionaries as an unswerving defender of civil liberties. Hence in May 1791 the National Assembly issued a decree for the writer's remains to be brought back to Paris and interred in the Panthéon, as its second resident after Mirabeau. Voltaire was given a grandiose state funeral on 11 July 1791, attended by hundreds of thousands of Parisians, involving a huge cortege accompanied by a poem by André Chénier's younger brother Marie-Joseph set to the music of François-Joseph Gossec. In turn, André Chénier contrasts the consecration of the celebrated champion of public freedoms, social order and religious toleration with the self-serving demagogues promoting the shabbier spectacle of forty Swiss mutineers paraded through the streets of Paris in April 1792.

Z

Zeus. In ancient Greek religion, Zeus was the god of the sky and of thunder. He ruled as king of the gods on Mount Olympus. Born of the most illustrious line of elemental gods and Titans, he was traditionally married to Hera, queen of Olympus and goddess of women, marriage and childbirth. Many myths recount Zeus's amorous extra-marital adventures fathering sundry other gods and demi-gods. The chief symbols of his power were the thunderbolt, the eagle and the bull.

CHRONOLOGY OF
ANDRÉ CHÉNIER AND FAMILY

❖

Pre-Revolution

1762. 30 October. Baptism of André-Marie Chénier in the Catholic church of Galata, Constantinople (Istanbul). His father, Louis Chénier (1722–95), was co-manager and representative of the Lavabre et Dussol textile company from Marseille. Louis had ambitions to go into diplomacy. André's mother, Élisabeth Lomaca (1729?–1808), of Turkish-Greek origin, flamboyantly assumed her Greek heritage in both dress and culture throughout her life. André was the seventh child, although only three elder children survived, including Louis-Sauveur (1761–1823) who would become a general under the revolutionary Republic and the Napoleonic Empire.

1764. 11 February. Baptism of the Chéniers' last child, Marie-Joseph-Blaise (d. 1811), his mother's favourite and future poet-playwright and politician in the Revolution.

1765. The Chénier family returns to France (April-May). André and an elder brother lodge with their aunt, Marie Béraud, in Carcassonne. Their father finally gets a diplomatic post as *consul général* in Morocco (first posting 1767–73).

1773. Louis Chénier returns to France in September and brings André to Paris. With his brothers, he becomes a boarder at the aristocratic Collège de Navarre.

1774. The Chéniers move to the Marais district (in today's rue de Sévigné) where the mother, 'La belle Grecque', regularly hosts an orientalized salon for artists, writers and worldly acquaintances, including some foreign dignitaries.

1778. Chénier wins French and Latin prizes in Rhetoric at school, beating the young Camille Desmoulins to the Latin prize. Composes his first fragments of epic and bucolic verse, imitations of Homer and Virgil respectively.

1762 ▪ ▪ ▪ ▪

1763 ▪ ▪ ▪ ▪

1764 ▪ ▪ ▪ ▪

1765 ▪ ▪ ▪ ▪

1766 ▪ ▪ ▪ ▪

1771 ▪ ▪ ▪ ▪

1773 ▪ ▪ ▪ ▪

1774 ▪ ▪ ▪ ▪

1775 ▪ ▪ ▪ ▪

1778 ▪ ▪ ▪ ▪

CHRONOLOGY OF
REVOLUTIONARY FRANCE

❖

Pre-Revolution

■ ■ ■ 1762

1762. Louis XV has ruled France since coming of age in 1723. He has squandered his initial popularity by alienating the Parlements with tax reform and anti-*philosophe* policies in the 1750s and by embroiling France in a costly and disastrous war in 1756.

■ ■ ■ 1763

1763. The Treaty of Paris ends the Seven Years War (1756-1763) that saw the new alliance of France and Austria defeated and humiliated by Great Britain and Prussia. France loses important colonial territories in North America and India.

■ ■ ■ 1764

1764. The Jesuit order is expelled from France.

■ ■ ■ 1765

1765. Death of the Dauphin, son of Louis XV.

■ ■ ■ 1766

1766. Escalation of a power struggle between the king and the regional law courts in France, the Parlements, over sovereignty and taxation.

■ ■ ■ 1771

1771. The government led by Chancellor Maupeou introduces sweeping judicial reform to strengthen the power of the king against the judiciary. The Parlement de Paris is sent into exile and replaced.

■ ■ ■ 1773

■ ■ ■ 1774

1774. Death of Louis XV. He is succeeded by his 19-year-old grandson, who becomes Louis XVI. The new king restores the Parlements and appoints a reformist ministry, including the *philosophe*-friendly Malesherbes and Turgot. Their laissez-faire economics are undone by bad harvests and food riots (the so-called Flour Wars of spring 1775) and by vested interests. Malesherbes resigns and Turgot is dismissed in 1776.

1775. American War of Independence. French funding and military support for the insurgents against Great Britain will put significant strain on state finances throughout 1780s.

■ ■ ■ 1775

■ ■ ■ 1778

1778. Deaths of Voltaire (30 May) and Rousseau (2 July).

1779–80. Final two years in school, studying philosophy as the last part of his humanities curriculum.

1781. Chénier obtains a legal certificate attesting to his 'nobility' with a view to embarking on a military career. However, rules on qualifying as a 'noble' had been tightened up earlier in the year, thereby thwarting his application for a commission in December. He throws himself into the world of pleasure in Paris, writing love poetry to an Opéra actress whom he calls 'Lycoris'. Starts *Art d'aimer* on the model of Ovid's *Ars amatoria*. Becomes acquainted with the neo-classical poet Ponce-Denis Écouchard Lebrun who admires Chénier's talents.

1782. The poet plans to join an imminent diplomatic mission to the Middle East led by the comte de Choiseul-Gouffier. Meanwhile he joins the Angoumois regiment in Strasbourg as a simple unpaid volunteer (June–October). In winter, he suffers from painful bouts of kidney stones (lithiasis) which would recur intermittently throughout his life.

1784. Chénier writes some verses on the new 'aérostats', part of the 'balloon-mania' gripping France. First sketches for his great philosophical poem 'Hermès', which would remain unfinished despite occasional bouts of enthusiasm for it over the next few years. Same pattern for the projected and unfinished epic poem on the New World, 'L'Amérique', begun about this time. His plan to travel to Turkey with Choiseul-Gouffier having fallen through, Chénier visits Switzerland with the Trudaine brothers (September–November). In Zurich, he meets the physiognomist Johann Kaspar Lavater.

1785. A year of study, poetry and a love affair with Michelle de Bonneuil, the 'Camille' of his *Élégies*. Deeply affected by a visit to the disused prison cells at the fort of Vincennes, Chénier champions a more humane form of political justice.

1786. Chénier receives verses from Jean-Pierre Claris de Florian about the abuses of despotic rule and the Inquisition in Spain. He befriends the antiquarian Pierre-François Hugues d'Hancarville and the artist Jacques-Louis David. In June he stays with the Trudaine brothers in Montigny and writes 'Épître sur des ouvrages'. The poet becomes one of many admirers of the Anglo-Italian artist Maria Cosway, then living in Paris. Plans are made for a two-year journey to the Middle-East with the Trudaine brothers. Chénier gets as far as Rome before returning via Nice early in the following year.

1787. He writes the pastoral dialogue 'La Liberté' (March) and the indignant 'Hymne à la justice' (May), two poems with clear political messages. Chénier meets the Italian poet Vittorio Alfieri and, with the Polish poet Julian Ursyn Niemcewicz, becomes a member of the artists' circle around Maria Cosway and David. In November he takes up the post of personal secretary to the chevalier (later marquis) de La Luzerne, newly appointed French ambassador to Great Britain. He travels to London with Mrs Cosway.

• • • • 1779

• • • • 1781

1781. The Swiss banker and Minister of Finance, Jacques Necker, publishes his *Compte rendu*, a misleading account of the state finances that obscures the dire position of the French economy and encourages further borrowing.

• • • • 1782

• • • • 1783

• • • • 1784

1783–86. Necker's replacement as Minister of Finance, Calonne, discovers the severity of the national deficit. However, his increasingly drastic proposals for fiscal reform are ultimately rejected and he is dismissed in 1787.

• • • • 1785

1785–86. The Diamond Necklace Affair confirms public opinion of Marie-Antoinette's profligacy, even though she is innocent of any involvement in the scam practised on the court jewellers.

• • • • 1786

• • • • 1787

1787. An Assembly of Notables meets to deal with the growing financial crisis in France. The assembly fails to agree on solutions and is dissolved.

1788. Correspondence with his ambitious younger brother Marie-Joseph. Chénier returns to Paris with the marquis de La Luzerne (July–November) where he is close to d'Hancarville and Alfieri. In late November he returns to his embassy posting in London.

Revolution

1789. 3 April. Excluded from a worldly gathering at the French embassy, Chénier dines alone in Hood's Tavern, Covent Garden, and pens bitter reflections on the snobbery and prejudice of his so-called 'superiors'.

15 June. Marie-Joseph drafts an appeal for an end to theatre censorship, *De la liberté du théâtre en France*, which is published in July.

14 July. Louis-Sauveur Chénier encourages rebellion in the name of the king's liberal cousin the duc d'Orléans and participates in the storming of the Bastille. These Orléanist sympathies will be mistakenly attributed to André when he is denounced to the revolutionary authorities in 1794.

August. Chénier returns to Paris, possibly to see off his sister who sets sail with her husband, a military commander, for the Île de France (Mauritius).

4 November. Immense success of Marie-Joseph's long-banned political tragedy *Charles IX ou La Saint-Barthélemy* at the Comédie-Française.
19 November. Chénier returns to London at the request of the marquis de La Luzerne, escorting the diplomatic bag.

1790. 12 April. Founding of the liberal political club La Société de 1789, meeting in the Palais-Royal. The Trudaines and François de Pange enrol Chénier in its members' list, with the note 'in England'.

July. Chénier returns to Paris, possibly on a diplomatic mission to General Lafayette or as private escort to Mrs Cosway on her way to Italy.
14 July. Chénier sketches out a comedy in the manner of Aristophanes

1788 ••••

1789 ••••

June

July

August

October

November

December

1790 ••••

June
July

•••• 1788   **1788.** Convergence of subsistence crisis (bad harvests, soaring prices), financial crisis (ballooning state debt, fiscal chaos) and political crisis (no representation of middle and lower orders of society). The king orders a meeting of the États-Généraux (the Estates-General).

Revolution

•••• 1789   **1789. 5 May.** Representatives of the three orders (clergy, nobility, commoners) of the Estates-General convene at Versailles. This body last met in 1614. The third-estate numbers are doubled but voting is still by estate. Stalemate.

June   **20 June.** Serment du Jeu de Paume (The Tennis-Court Oath). The representatives of the third estate, joined by some renegade priests and nobles, constitute themselves as the National Assembly and swear to remain assembled until they have provided France with a new constitution.

July   **11 July.** The popular finance minister Jacques Necker is dismissed. There is widespread public anxiety and unrest in Paris.

14 July. Frightened inhabitants of Paris search for weapons to defend themselves against a rumoured attack by royalist troops. Fall of the Bastille.

August   **July-August.** La Grande Peur (The Great Fear). Rioting and attacks on seigneurial properties in the provinces, fuelled by rumours of an aristocratic 'famine plot' to starve the people into submission, or false stories of brigands, even foreign troops, destroying crops and homes.

4 August. The new National Assembly abolishes 'feudalism' and seigneurial 'privileges'.

26 August. Déclaration des droits de l'homme et du citoyen (Declaration of the Rights of Man and the Citizen) adopted and published by the National Assembly.

October   **5–6 October.** Journées d'octobre (October Days). Women march on Versailles to demand lower food prices. They force the royal family, followed by the National Assembly, to move to Paris.

November   **2 November.** Church property is nationalized.

December   **12 December.** Bonds raised against the Church lands are introduced. These *assignats* become a form of inflationary legal tender in the course of the next few years.

•••• 1790   **1790. 13 February.** Most religious orders are suppressed.

June   **19 June.** Hereditary titles of nobility are abolished.

July   **12 July.** Constitution Civile du Clergé (Civil Constitution of the Clergy) is passed by the National Assembly, making the Catholic Church a subordinate branch of the revolutionary state.

entitled *La Liberté*, in mock-honour of the Fête de la Fédération assembling some 300,000 people in the Champ-de-Mars on the first anniversary of the fall of the Bastille.

28 August. Chénier publishes his first and most successful piece of revolutionary journalism, the long article 'Avis au Peuple français sur ses véritables ennemis' in the *Mémoires de la Société de 1789* (no. 13). The work is also published as a widely circulated pamphlet. It warns of divisive demagoguery and Jacobin agitators. It is denounced by Camille Desmoulins in his news-sheet *Révolutions de France et de Brabant* (no. 41).

8 September. Chénier writes to the honorary secretary of the French embassy in London, François-Marie Barthélemy, to ask for the return to France of his effects and books.

2 November. Chénier receives a medal *Bene meritis* from the King of Poland for his 'Avis au peuple français' which the Polish monarch has had translated into Polish.

1791. 2 March. Chénier sends to Lebrun his Pindaric ode 'Le Jeu de Paume. À Louis David, peintre'. One of only two poems published in the poet's lifetime, it is inspired by David's pen and sepia drawing of the event exhibited in the artist's studio (May-June) and at the Salon (August-September).

3 March. Chénier finishes his political pamphlet *Réflexions sur l'esprit de parti* which attacks both revolutionary and counter-revolutionary agitators. It would be published in early April.

25–30 April. Angered by the increasing number of public disturbances and anti-clerical attacks, Chénier writes the perceptive article 'Les Autels de la peur' about the growing function of fear in revolutionary politics, although it remains unpublished in his lifetime.

5 June. The *Moniteur universel* publishes Chénier's open letter to the 'philosophe' Guillaume-Thomas Raynal, criticizing him for reneging on his enlightened politics in not supporting the 'Déclaration des droits de l'homme et du citoyen' and other progressive legislation adopted by the National Assembly. This is the first of a number of polemical interventions that Chénier would make in this widely-circulating news-sheet.

July–August. In the wake of the royal family's failed attempt to flee Paris, the Jacobin Club splits between radicals and moderates over how to respond to this dereliction of monarchical duty, with the latter forming the more conservative Club des Feuillants (16 July). Chénier registers as a member of the Feuillants with his friends de Pange and the Trudaine brothers.

1790 ▪ ▪ ▪ ▪
July

August

September

1791 ▪ ▪ ▪ ▪

February
March

April

June

July

August

▪ ▪ ▪ ▪ 1790   **14 July.** Fête de la Fédération (Festival of Federation) marking the first
July   anniversary of the Fall of the Bastille. King, Church leaders and the
    National Guard swear allegiance to the Revolution.
August   **August.** Mutiny in the army barracks at Nancy over pay. The royalist
    General Bouillé violently suppresses the mutiny. The mutinous Swiss
    soldiers of the Châteauvieux regiment are severely punished. They will
    later be rehabilitated by the National Assembly and hailed as martyrs of
    revolutionary liberty by the Jacobin Club.

September

    27 November. Decree compelling priests to swear an oath of allegiance
    to the Civil Constitution of the Clergy.

▪ ▪ ▪ ▪ 1791   **1791. 3 January.** Roll-call of all priests to take the oath to the Civil
    Constitution of the Clergy.
February   **20 February.** The king's pious aunts flee to Rome.
March

    10 March. The Pope condemns the Civil Constitution of the Clergy.
April

June   **20–21 June.** La Fuite à Varennes (the royal family's 'flight' or attempted
    escape from Paris halted at Varennes). Responses to the king's 'abduction'
    or 'treachery' polarize opinions.

July   **17 July.** Massacre du Champ de Mars (Champ de Mars Massacre).
    National Guards open fire on crowds massing to sign a petition to have
    the king deposed.
August   **22 August.** Uprising of slaves in the richest French colony of Saint-
    Domingue. This will lead to twelve years of revolution, the abolition of
    slavery in the French territories (1794–1802) and the institution of the first
    freed–slave Republic of Haiti on 1 January 1804.

14 September. The marquis de La Luzerne dies, severing Chénier's last nominal tie with the London embassy but leaving him without employment.

22 October. The *Moniteur universel* publishes Chénier's letter deploring the Revolution's increasingly violent anti-clericalism, calling instead for a separation of Church and State.

16 November. He votes for the moderate Lafayette in the elections for mayor of Paris. Lafayette loses to the Jacobin Jérôme Pétion.

24 December. A letter from Louis Chénier to his daughter Hélène reveals how the family is riven politically: his mother and Marie-Joseph support the radical Left; his father and André, the moderate Right, the so-called 'friends of law and order'.

1792. 9 February. Première of Marie-Joseph's *Caïus Gracchus* at the Théâtre Français, receiving a stormy reception from different political factions.

16 February. Chénier publishes a withering critique in the *Journal de Paris* of the Jacobin Pierre Manuel's new edition of Mirabeau's letters. A welter of polemical articles by Chénier follow in the same news-sheet: attacking mayor Pétion and the Jacobins and claiming that the middle orders of society are 'la masse du vrai Peuple' (26 February); recalling David to his work as the leading exponent of history painting (24 March); decrying the indiscipline in the revolutionary armies sent to war with Austria and Prussia (5 May); more virulent anti-Jacobin broadsides appear (29 April, 11 May, 3 June, 14 June, 27 June); an appeal for national unity around the king and the constitution (5 July); an appeal to the National Assembly to root out Jacobin subversion and refuse the call-up of 20,000 'fédérés' soldiers from the provinces into Paris (10 July); a final attack ad hominem on the war-mongering journalist and *député* Jacques Pierre Brissot in which Chénier declares that he is 'ready to die' in defence of the constitution and its legally established political order (27 July).

28 February. Marie-Joseph publishes a public defence of the Jacobins of which he is a member and so starts a public quarrel with his older brother that will become increasingly vitriolic over the year.

28 March. Chénier reacts violently and repeatedly to the Swiss mutiny, in a series of in articles published on 29 March, 4 April, 10 April and 13 April, to what he sees as an affront to the legal order and as the consecration of mob rule. On the day of the festival itself (15 April) he publishes the bitterly ironic 'Hymne sur l'entrée triomphale des Suisses révoltés du régiment de Châteauvieux, fêtés à Paris sur une motion de Collot-d'Herbois'. This is only the second poem to appear in his lifetime, and it will be the last. It is also among the first of his iambics.

• • • • 1791	**27 August**. Declaration of Pillnitz. A joint Austrian-Prussian declaration in defence of Louis XVI and against the Revolution.
September	**14 September**. The king signs the Constitution and is restored to his functions.
October	**1 October**. Legislative Assembly, elected to take over from first 'Constituant' National Assembly, convenes for the first time. **17 October**. Counter-revolutionaries are massacred in unrest at Avignon.
November	**November**. Decrees issued against both émigré nobles and non-juring priests, which the king tries to veto but is overruled by the National Assembly.
December	
• • • • 1792 February	**1792. 9 February**. Property of émigrés declared forfeit to the nation.
March	**10 March**. Nomination of a war-mongering ministry, drawn mainly from the 'Girondin' camp of republican sympathizers. **23 March**. Start of the affair of Les Suisses de Châteauvieux in which forty-one Swiss soldiers sentenced to the galleys for a violent mutiny against their army commanders in August 1790 were amnestied by the National Assembly in December 1791 after an appeal by the Jacobin Jean-Marie Collot d'Herbois. 'Liberated' from the prison in Brest, the Swiss soldiers become the heroes of a 'fête de la Liberté' proposed and organized in Paris by the Jacobins.

1–6 August. As Paris simmers with imminent republican insurrection, Chénier travels to Forges-les-Eaux in Normandy with Michel Trudaine and his mistress. A late *bucolique* is written there, 'Fille du vieux pasteur'.

8 August. Hearing of a possible plan to thwart a republican uprising in the capital, Chénier writes to the justice minister Étienne de Joly to offer his services. In preparation for a meeting with the minister the following day, he drafts a speech to be read by Louis XVI before the National Assembly. Either denied entry to the ministry or not heeded, Chénier returns home, dejected and ill, to sit out the popular insurrection that overthrows the monarchy on 10 August.

11 August. Knowing himself to be a likely target for republican reprisals, Chénier leaves Paris, retreating most probably to friends in Versailles or Louveciennes.

10 September. The September Massacres (2–7 September) in the prisons of Paris spread to Versailles. He escapes to Rouen via Forges-les-Eaux, arriving on 12 September.

17–26 September. Chénier undertakes a mysterious trip to Le Havre under the alias 'Antoine Caun' and dines with a number of unnamed acquaintances.

20 September. Marie-Joseph takes his seat in the Convention as the new *député* for Seine-et-Oise.

28 October. Chénier returns from Rouen to Paris. He claims to have withdrawn from society to devote himself to studying the Classics but may already be planning to contribute to a defence of Louis XVI who is soon to go on trial.

• • • • 1792   **20 April**. War declared on Austria. When Prussia comes to Austria's
April   defence, war is also declared on Prussia.
June   **19 June**. The French war effort is failing, but Louis XVI vetoes the call-
               up of provincial troops to Paris.
               20 June. Revolutionary militants, mainly urban labourers and artisans
               known as 'sans-culottes', invade the Tuileries palace and threaten Louis
               XVI.
July   **25 July**. Brunswick Manifesto issued by Austria and Prussia warning of
               dire consequences for the French people if any harm were to come to the
               royal family. It galvanizes republican resistance.
               25–30 July. Arrival of the provincial troops, the *fédérés*, from Brest and
               Marseille (the latter popularizing La Marseillaise).
August

               9 August. Insurrectionary commune formed in Paris.
               10 August. Storming of the Tuileries palace and overthrow of the
               monarchy. The royal family take refuge in the National Assembly.

               23 August. Longwy falls to the Prussians who will take Verdun on 2
               September.
September   **2–7 September**. Massacres de septembre (Mob massacre of suspected
               counter-revolutionary prisoners in Parisian prisons).

               20 September. First republican army victory at Valmy.
               21 September. The Convention (new National Assembly) meets for first
               time.
               22 September. The French Republic declared by the Convention.
               The revolutionary calendar will be back-dated to this day when it is
               introduced in October 1793.
               2 October. Comité de Sûreté Générale (Committee of General Secu-
               rity) established. It is responsible for the internal policing of the state. In
October   September 1793 this Committee falls under the jurisdiction of the Com-
               mittee of Public Safety (see below) and works alongside it to implement
               the policies of the Terror, although not without tension and division.
               6 November. French victory of Jemappes. The republican army marches
               into the Austrian Netherlands (today Belgium).
               3 December. Trial begins of Louis XVI by the members of the
               Convention.

17 December. After Louis XVI's first appearance before the Convention (11 December), his legal defence team take on the talented lawyer Raymond de Sèze who in turn secretively employs Chénier to help formulate his case.

25 December. He publishes an unsigned letter in the *Mercure* arguing that the king can only be tried in accordance with the prevailing Constitution of 1791 which grants him inviolability from prosecution. A further letter in a more concessionary vein, but still arguing for the king's acquittal, is published in the same news-sheet on 29 December.

1793. Early January. Chénier drafts an address, presumably for publication as a pamphlet, and a speech for an unnamed *député*, both supporting the Girondins' call for a popular national vote on Louis XVI's fate. The idea of a popular vote is rejected by the Convention (15 January). He then writes a letter to be read in the name of the king to the Convention demanding the popular vote, but de Sèze chooses not to use it.

16–17 January. In the public roll-call of *députés* to declare their vote on the death penalty for Louis XVI, Marie-Joseph votes reluctantly for the king's execution.

24 January. Disgusted with the king's execution and alienated from his younger brother, Chénier appears to have retired to Passy where friends give him lodgings.

8 March. Louis-Sauveur is appointed as *Adjudant-Général* in the Armée du Nord. He will be removed from his post in September and placed under house arrest as a former noble.

17 March. As mass conscription is enforced, Chénier is exempted from military service on health grounds and he hands in his national guard uniform to his Section.

1 April. Thanks to his father who is active in his own revolutionary Section, Chénier obtains a *certificat de civisme* (paper identifying him as a good citizen) and a pass to leave Paris. He retires to Versailles and lives in lodgings opposite the royal park which he often crosses to see his friends in Louveciennes, including Françoise 'Fanny' Lecouteulx with whom he is secretly in love.

May–June. He pens a number of melancholic and poignant 'Odes à Fanny'.

1792 ▪ ▪ ▪ ▪
November
December

1793 ▪ ▪ ▪ ▪
January

February

March

April

May

June

▪ ▪ ▪ ▪ 1792
November
December

▪ ▪ ▪ ▪ 1793   **1793. 15 January.** Louis XVI found guilty of treason.
January   **17 January.** Vote on the king's fate narrowly sentences him to death.

21 January. Louis XVI is guillotined in the place de la Révolution (today place de la Concorde).

February   **1 February.** War is declared against Great Britain and Holland.
                     7 February. War is declared on Spain.
March   **9 March.** Convention sends out *représentants-en-mission* (members of the Convention accompanying armed forces to internal and external fronts). Conscription introduced to levy 300,000 men. Two days later the Catholic and royalist Vendée region erupts in civil war.
                     10 March. Revolutionary Tribunal established.

April   **6 April.** Comité de Salut Public (Committee of Public Safety) established. It becomes the effective executive arm of revolutionary government over the next fifteen months.

May   **May-October.** Violent pro-royalist or pro-Girondin revolts against the Jacobin-led government in Paris, especially in the West and South.
June   **31 May-2 June.** Parliamentary purge of the Girondins from Convention. Rise of Montagnards (*députés* who are mainly Paris-based Jacobins).
                     24 June. Adoption of the republican Constitution of 1793, significantly increasing suffrage. It will be indefinitely suspended on 10 October in favour of a 'revolutionary government' until future peace. It will never be implemented.

July–August. Poems in Marat's honour by Audoin and Cubières-Palmézeaux published in late July and early August inspire Chénier to reply in iambics and especially in his powerful ode 'A Marie-Anne-Charlotte Corday' (started most probably 28 July).

10 August. On the first anniversary of the overthrow of the monarchy, David is charged with organizing a huge festival in celebration of 'La Réunion et l'Indivisibilité de la République'. Its plaster and pasteboard monuments and decorations depicting violent revolutionary events are mocked in Chénier's 'Fragment: Un vulgaire assassin va chercher les ténèbres'.

3 October. He visits Paris to put his papers in order with the authorities and, accompanying his father, visits the local revolutionary Section.

3–4 October. Chénier's fellow poet and anti-Jacobin journalist, Jean-Antoine Roucher, is arrested.

31 October. A decree of the Convention changing the name of the town Montmorency to 'Émile' in honour of Jean-Jacques Rousseau forms part of the impetus for Chénier to start work on his ode 'A Versailles'.

November. He works on a number of poems, mostly bitingly satirical odes, responding in large part to Marie-Joseph's much-applauded speech of 5 November on the need for secular republican festivals, as well as to his brother's later intervention (25 November) calling for Marat to be interred in the Panthéon in the place of the disgraced Mirabeau.

December. From his retreat in Versailles, Chénier scrutinizes news reports from Paris and pens a number of odes and iambics in response to revolutionary speeches and propaganda such as his formal Pindaric ode 'O mon esprit, au sein des cieux'.

1794. 28 January. Reacting to an account in the *Moniteur* of Bertrand Barère's bombastic call to 'popularize' French diction, Chénier writes scathing iambics to the Muses, 'On dit que le dédain froid et silencieux'.

31 January. The poet Roucher is transferred to Saint-Lazare prison.

11 February. The police agent for the Comité de Sûreté Générale (internal state security apparatus), Nicolas Guénot, starts investigating suspected counter-revolutionaries in Passy linked to Chénier.

7 March. Armed with a search warrant, Guénot makes an evening call on the house of Mme Piscatory in Passy. Chénier is caught leaving the building and asked to present his papers. He claims to be on his way back to Paris although he later contradicts himself in saying that he is escorting a female acquaintance back to Versailles. Under suspicion, he is

1793 ● ● ● ●
July

August

September

October

November

December

1794 ● ● ● ●
January

February

• • • • 1793 July	**13 July**. Marat assassinated in his bath by Charlotte Corday, who is guillotined on 17 July. **27 July**. Robespierre joins the Committee of Public Safety.
August	**23 August**. Decree of mass conscription, the *levée en masse*.
September	**5 September**. Under pressure from mobs, demagogues and the municipal Paris Commune, the Convention agrees to introduce 'government by terror'. Beginning of the so-called 'Terror'. **17 September**. Loi des Suspects (Law of Suspects) introduced, increasing arrests of alleged counter-revolutionaries. **29 September**. Law of 'Le Maximum général' introduced, putting a price ceiling on necessities to curb galloping inflation, speculation on the *assignats*, and food-hoarding.
October	**16 October**. Marie-Antoinette is guillotined. **31 October**. Execution of Girondin leaders.
November	**10 November**. As part of the prevailing de-Christianizing movement in the Terror, the Fête de la Raison (Festival of Reason) is held in Notre-Dame.
December	**December**. Successful counter-offensive by republican armies. Toulon is retaken from the British.
• • • • 1794 January	
February	**1794. 4 February**. Abolition of slavery in the French colonies, partly on revolutionary principle, partly in recognition of the balance of power in Saint-Domingue and to turn the insurgent freed slaves into allies against the British and Spanish.

held overnight in Mme Piscatory's house until an arrest warrant can be produced against him.

8 March. Chénier is interrogated by Guénot and his evasive and mocking answers, as well as his refusal to sign a written statement, confirm his arrest on the catch-all 'grounds of state security'. The next day he is transferred to Paris and incarcerated in Saint-Lazare prison.

16 March. Aimée Franquetot de Coigny and her lover Casimir de Montrond are locked up in Saint-Lazare. Inmates have the freedom to mingle inside the prison and Chénier mixes with their aristocratic circle.

6–8 May. Thorough searches are made throughout Saint-Lazare by police administrators, terrifying the prisoners who have no contact with the outside world except to receive food and laundry. It is most likely at this point that Chénier composes his ode 'La Jeune Captive', lending poetic voice to Aimée de Coigny's imagined fears and hopes.

20 May. Without consulting Marie-Joseph, Louis Chénier addresses a letter to the prisons' commission naively drawing their attention to André's anti-Jacobin journalism. He exacerbates this misjudged initiative by approaching the hard-line member of the Comité de Salut Public, Barère, for help. (Three days before Chénier's eventual execution, Barère was alleged to have given Louis the devastatingly cynical response: 'Votre fils sortira dans trois jours' — 'Your son will be out of prison in three days'.)

22 May. Marie-Joseph makes some tentative enquiries about securing the release of his elder brother Louis-Sauveur who had been imprisoned in the Conciergerie since March after attacking in writing a revolutionary representative in the army. This move brings Marie-Joseph under further suspicion, possibly reducing his room for manoeuvre to plead André's case.

26 May. The Comité de Sûreté Générale gives an official order to the concierge at Saint-Lazare to keep Chénier in prison until further notice.

8 June. The grandiose Fête de l'Être Suprême drives Chénier to draft a number of withering iambics which are smuggled out to his family concealed in his laundry packets.

• • • • 1794
March

24 **March**. The extremist faction grouped around the journalist Jacques-René Hébert are guillotined.

April

5 **April**. The 'indulgent' faction grouped around the Jacobin *député* Georges-Jacques Danton are guillotined.

May

June

8 **June**. Fête de l'Être Suprême (Festival of the Supreme Being), a deist festival inspired by Robespierre's readings of Jean-Jacques Rousseau and orchestrated by the artist Jacques-Louis David.

10 **June**. Law of 22 Prairial (this day's date in the revolutionary calendar), simplifying and speeding up the judicial process with only verdicts of acquittal or death allowed. Notable increase in numbers convicted and executed.

26 **June**. Battle of Fleurus. Decisive victory of the French republican forces over the First Coalition of European monarchies against them.

1 **July**. Robespierre gives a speech at the Jacobin Club denouncing a conspiracy against him in the National Convention and the Committees of Public Safety and General Security.

11 July. Chénier and Roucher figure on the list.

17 July. Chénier's fellow prisoner, the artist Joseph-Benoît Suvée, paints the famous last portrait of André.

23 July. Chénier waits in anguish as the first batch (*fournée*) of twenty-five prisoners is called out at 6 am. He is not named in this group. But knowing that this is only a short reprieve, he writes up his remaining iambics and other verse on three narrow strips of paper, then folds and conceals them in packets to be returned to his family the following day.
24 July. The tumbrils return to Saint-Lazare at 3.30 pm. Twenty-seven prisoners are called out in this infamous second *fournée*, starting with Roucher and Chénier. At 6.30 pm they are taken to the Conciergerie to await trial. Each prisoner receives his or her own bill of indictment. Chénier's cites his persistent anti-Jacobin journalism of 1791 and 1792 but also confuses him with his older brother Louis-Sauveur in stating that he defamed a revolutionary official in the army.
25 July. Chénier is among the prisoners appearing before the Revolutionary Tribunal. One further charge presented to the jury singles him out as the author of an attack on 'la fête des Châteauvieux' (of 15 April 1792).

Roucher and Chénier are the last prisoners of the day to be guillotined. Marie-Joseph finds out about his brother's execution in the *Journal du soir* and tells his family the tragic news.

8 July. French forces under Jourdan and Pichegru capture Brussels.

11 July. As part of a trumped-up 'prisons' conspiracy' that was first attributed to the Luxembourg prison with the principal aim of expediting inmates to the guillotine, the police administrators batten on Saint-Lazare, interrogate its detainees and their own infiltrated police spies in order to draw up a list of over sixty prisoners to be eliminated. Chénier and Roucher figure on the list.

14 July. At Robespierre's insistence, the brutal représentant-en-mission, Fouché, is excluded from the Jacobin Club. An unholy alliance of moderates and extremists start to plot Robespierre's downfall.

20 July. A definitive list of eighty-two names is processed by the public prosecutor's office where the chief state prosecutor Antoine-Quentin Fouquier-Tinville blithely adds further accusations to the charge sheet from Saint-Lazare.

25 July. The prisoners appear together before the Revolutionary Tribunal. They are indicted, judged and found guilty collectively, although two are excused because of mistaken identity.

At 3 pm, the twenty-five condemned (twenty-two men and three women, plus three other women from the previous *journée* who had feigned pregnancy) are taken to the site of execution at the Barrière du Trône-Renversé (today place de l'Île-de-la-Réunion in eastern Paris) where the executions start at 4 pm and finish at 6 pm.

All the bodies are then dumped in the communal grave dug in the garden of the former Picpus convent which will ultimately hold more than 1,300 victims of the Terror.

26 July. A third *journée* of prisoners from Saint-Lazare are tried and executed, including the Trudaine brothers.

27 July. Robespierre and his followers are shouted down in the Convention and arrested. Abolition of the Paris Commune. Closure of the Jacobin Club.

1794 ▪ ▪ ▪ ▪
July

1 August. When the authorities come to seize what remains of Chénier's   August
belongings in the name of the state, Louis informs them that his son
possessed only the bedding and books that he took to Saint-Lazare.
3 October. Aimée de Coigny and Montrond are released from Saint-   October
Lazare. They get married in January the following year.

November
December

1795. 9 January. Chénier's former political ally and fellow prisoner   1795 ▪ ▪ ▪ ▪
Pierre-Louis Ginguené publishes the poet's ode 'La Jeune Captive' in the   January
influential review *La Décade philosophique, littéraire et politique.* The poem
is widely appreciated and admired.

February
April

25 May. Death of Louis Chénier.   May

14 July. Certain moderate and conservative news-sheets and periodicals   July
begin a campaign of harassment against Marie-Joseph, publicly intimating
that he could have saved his brother from the guillotine but chose not
to do so. The royalist wit Antoine Rivarol makes a cutting biblical
reference to Marie-Joseph as 'le frère d'Abel Chénier'. Marie-Joseph will
reply with the eloquent 'Épître sur la Calomnie' published in December.
However, the campaign of public denigration continues unabated.

August

October

1796. Françoise 'Fanny' Lecouteulx dies of pulmonary tuberculosis (8   1796 ▪ ▪ ▪ ▪
January).

• • • • 1794 July	**28 July.** Execution of Robespierre and his close political allies, such as Louis-Antoine Saint-Just and Georges Couthon. Their deaths mark the end of the Terror and these two days (27–28 July) are referred to as 'Thermidor' after the corresponding dates of 9–10 Thermidor in the revolutionary calendar. Repeal of the Law of 22 Prairial.
August	**31 July-10 August.** Reorganization of the Committee of Public Safety and the Revolutionary Tribunal.
October	
November	**12 November.** The Jacobin Club is dissolved.
December	**24 December.** The Law of 'Le Maximum' is abolished.
• • • • 1795 January	
February	**21 February.** Decree separating Church and State.
April	**1 April.** Insurrection of Germinal (named after the revolutionary calendar month), rioting and protest by lower social orders against exorbitant food prices and economic stagnation. Unrest is quashed and remaining prominent Montagnards are imprisoned or deported.
	5 April. Peace treaty signed with Prussia.
	16 April. Peace treaty with Holland signed.
May	**20–23 May.** Insurrection of Prairial (named after the revolutionary calendar month), a more protracted and violent uprising calling for 'bread and the Constitution of 1793'. Its causes are the same as in April. It is ruthlessly put down and the sans-culottes disarmed and dispersed as a radical popular force.
July	**22 July.** Peace treaty signed with Spain.
August	**22 August.** Convention approves the Constitution of 1795, with restricted suffrage based on property-owning and wealth.
October	**4–6 October.** A large royalist force marches on Paris and is finally repulsed and defeated by republican troops under the young general Napoléon Bonaparte. The Napoleonic legend is launched.
	26 October. The Convention is dissolved. The new government of the Directory is inaugurated.

★   ★   ★   ★   ★

1801. Publication in the *Mercure de France* (22 March) of Chénier's poem   1801 ▪ ▪ ▪ ▪
initially given the title of 'Élégie dans le goût ancien', better known to
posterity as 'La Jeune Tarentine'. The poem is much admired and revives
interest in Chénier's poetry.

1808. Death of Élisabeth Chénier (6 November) at the home of her   1808 ▪ ▪ ▪ ▪
favourite son, Marie-Joseph.

1811. Death of Marie-Joseph Chénier (10 January) after a long illness.   1811 ▪ ▪ ▪ ▪

1812. Publication in the *Journal de Paris* of large extracts from Chénier's   1812 ▪ ▪ ▪ ▪
'Le Mendiant', indicating that there is still considerable interest in his
unpublished work.

1819. Publication of the first *Œuvres complètes* of André Chénier edited   1819 ▪ ▪ ▪ ▪
by Henri de Latouche (28 August). Far from definitive, this work will
nonetheless establish Chénier's posthumous reputation and begin an
ongoing debate over the scope and coherence of his *œuvre*. An abridged
Poésies d'André Chénier brought out by the same editor the following year
will only add to the poet's growing influence.

*This biographical notice is deeply indebted to the detailed 'Chronologie'
provided in Chénier, Œuvres poétiques, I, 31–99.*

SUGGESTIONS FOR USE OF
CHÉNIER'S POEMS IN THE CLASSROOM

❖

Select and adapt the suggested exercises below according to the level of French-language proficiency of the class.

Set one of the poems to music. Choose any style: classical, folk, jazz, rock, rap. Use an old tune or compose a new one. See if the musical setting of the poem changes significantly between its text in French and in English. How does the musical setting affect your reading or recitation of the poem? Why?

As a small-group exercise, choose one of the poems in French and translate it into English prose. Compare your prose translation with the English verse translation and discuss the differences, both in meaning and sentence structure.

Short generative writing exercise. On the theme of one of the poems — e.g. fear of death, imprisonment, unspoken love, anger at injustice, meaning of revolution, tyranny — write *non-stop* for three minutes. Write anything down. You can repeat yourself as much as you wish. The important thing is to keep going, not to stop. Read out your 'best' idea, expression or sentence to the class.

Emotional correlatives: in groups, discuss what act, image or expression most powerfully encapsulates for you one of the strong emotions articulated in Chénier's poems and their translations, e.g. terror, rage, love, freedom.

Look at how Chénier turns the Terror into a macabre pastoral (prisoners as sheep to be butchered) or Charlotte Corday into an avenging Greek goddess. Then retell an event or describe a character from the Revolution (or another historical period, including the present) by means of Greek mythology, religious parable, or folk/fairy tale. What insights, if any, does this give you of the event or character in question?

Choose one of the translations in English. Without looking at the source text, (re) translate the poem back into French, then compare your French retranslation with Chénier's 'original' poem.

Research exercise: carry out research into the historical and social geography of one or more of the poems, e.g. Saint-Lazare prison, Versailles, Louveciennes, Panthéon etc., and create an online map of Chénier's 'psychogeography' from these last poems.

What would a revolution look like in your classroom? How would you organize its aftermath to maintain your new revolutionary regime? Can Chénier's poems help you with your decisions here?

Write a critique of Chénier's politics from one of the following positions, or an 'intersectional' combination of them, citing specific poems in your critique:

Chénier is a 'bourgeois' poet defending the interests of his class;

Chénier is a sexist poet who reinforces masculine domination in his poems;

Chénier is a snob, an elitist poet, whose cultural references exclude the less-educated from understanding his work.

In groups or individually, copy out a poem in different colours and/or fonts to stress the intellectual or emotional emphases in the verse, as you read it. Then explain your choices.

Recitation exercises:

Alternate reading of the French and English versions of a poem, one line at a time, as consecutive translation; then again, one stanza at a time, where appropriate;

Read one of the poems in French or English, starting with a single speaker for the first line and with each subsequent line a second, third, fourth etc. speaker joins in the recitation to form a chorus;

Record your reading of the poem (in French and/or English) and play it back. What do the sounds tell us about the poem's meaning? Where do you put your emphases and why? Do the stress-points change when you read the poem with two or more speakers?

Learn one of the poems off by heart. Recite it to the class, then explain the process by which you learned it by heart and how you chose to cadence its reading.

SELECT BIBLIOGRAPHY

❖

Works by André Chénier

CHÉNIER, ANDRÉ, *De l'utopie à la Terreur: œuvres politiques complètes* (Paris: Le Trident, 1989)
—— *Œuvres complètes*, ed. by Gérard Walter (Paris: Gallimard, 1950)
—— *Œuvres en prose*, ed. by Louis Moland (Paris: Garnier Frères, 1879)
—— *Œuvres poétiques*, ed. by Georges Buisson and Édouard Guitton, 2 vols (Orléans: Paradigme, 2005–10)
—— *Poems*, ed. by Francis Scarfe (Oxford: Basil Blackwell, 1961)
—— *Poésies*, ed. by Louis Becq de Fouquières (Paris: Gallimard, 1994)

Secondary Works

APTER, EMILY, *The Translation Zone: A New Comparative Literature* (Princeton, NJ: Princeton University Press, 2006)
ARASSE, DANIEL, *La Guillotine et l'imaginaire de la Terreur* (Paris: Flammarion, 1987)
BERCOT, MARTINE, MICHEL COLLOT and CATRIONA SETH (eds), *Anthologie de la poésie française XVIIIe siècle, XIXe siècle, XXe siècle* (Paris: Gallimard, 2000)
BERMAN, MORRIS, *The Reenchantment of the World* (Ithaca, NY: Cornell University Press, 1981)
BLANNING, T. C. W., *The French Revolution: Aristocrats versus Bourgeois?* (Basingstoke: Macmillan Education, 1987)
BOULOISEAU, MARC, *Le Comité de Salut Public* (Paris: Presses universitaires de France, 1962)
BRIGGS, KATE, *This Little Art* (London: Fitzcarraldo, 2017)
BURT, E. S., 'Cracking the Code: The Poetical and Political Legacy of Chénier's "ANTIQUE VERSE"', *Yale French Studies*, 77 (1990), 210–42
BYRON, GEORGE GORDON NOEL, LORD, *Byron's Letters and Journals*, ed. by Leslie A. Marchand, 13 vols (London: John Murray, 1973–94)
CITTON, YVES, 'Imitation inventrice et harpe éolienne chez André Chénier: une théorisation de la productivité par l'Ailleurs', in *Ferments d'Ailleurs: transferts culturels entre Lumières et romantismes*, ed. by D. Bonnecase and F. Genton (Grenoble: ELLUG, 2010), pp. 35–77
COUDREUSE, ANNE, 'Élégie, souffle historique et pathétique dans la poésie d'André Chénier', in *Babel: Littératures plurielles*, 12 (2005), 79–90
Dictionnaire de l'Académie française, 5th edn, 2 vols (Paris: Smits et Cie, 1798)
DIDIER, BÉATRICE, *Écrire la Révolution 1789–1799* (Paris: Presses universitaires de France, 1989)
DOYLE, WILLIAM, *The French Revolution: A Very Short Introduction* (Oxford: Oxford University Press, 2001)
—— *The Oxford History of the French Revolution* (Oxford: Clarendon, 1989)
DURANTON, HENRI, 'Laclos a-t-il lu Proust?', in *Le Siècle de Voltaire: hommage à René Pomeau*, ed. by Christiane Mervaud and Sylvain Menant, 2 vols (Oxford: Voltaire Foundation, 1987), I, 449–56

FABRE, JEAN, *Chénier* (Paris: Hatier, 1965)

FONTVIEILLE-CORDANI, AGNÈS, 'Un vers brûlant d'amour et de larmes trempé: émotion et vers dans les *Élégies* d'André Chénier', in *L'Émotion poétique*, ed. by R. Bourkhis (Tunis: Sahar, 2010), pp. 117–36

GOULEMOT, JEAN M., and JEAN-JACQUES TATIN-GOURIER, *André Chénier: poésie et politique* (Paris: Minerve, 2005)

GRAMMONT, MAURICE, *Petit traité de versification française* (Paris: Armand Colin, 1965)

GRAVES, ROBERT, *Greek Myths* (London: QPD, 1991)

GUITTON, EDOUARD, 'L'Antiquité pour la modernité dans l'inspiration d'André Chénier', *Dix-huitième siècle*, 27 (1995), 191–99

LAHOUATI, GÉRARD, 'Un pèlerinage aux sources: éléments pour une poétique de l'eau chez André Chénier', in *Lectures d'André Chénier: Imitations et préludes poétiques, Art d'aimer, Élégies*, ed. by Jean-Noël Pascal (Rennes: Presses universitaires de Rennes, 2005), pp. 61–80

LAWRENCE, D. H., *The Complete Poems* (Ware: Wordsworth Editions, 1994)

LINTON, MARISA, *Choosing Terror: Virtue, Friendship, and Authenticity in the French Revolution* (Oxford: Oxford University Press, 2013)

LOMBEZ, CHRISTINE, 'Avec qui traduit-on? Les imaginaires de la traduction poétique', *Itinéraires*, 2018.2–3 (2019) <https://journals.openedition.org/itineraires/4561>

McCALLAM, DAVID, 'André Chénier's "dernières poésies": Animism and the Terror', *Forum for Modern Languages Studies*, 51.3 (July 2015), 304–15

—— 'Movement and Montage in André Chénier's *Ode à Versailles* (1793)', *Crossways Journal*, 1.1 (2017) <https://crossways.lib.uoguelph.ca/index.php/crossways/article/view/3883> [accessed 21 November 2020]

—— 'Orphée ou la poésie incarnée chez André Chénier', *Revue des littératures et des arts*, 17 (Autumn 2017) <https://revues.univ-pau.fr/opcit/278>

McGUINNESS, PATRICK (ed.), *French Poetry: From Medieval to Modern Times* (New York, London, & Toronto: Alfred A. Knopf, 2017)

McPHEE, PETER, *The French Revolution 1789–1799* (Oxford: Oxford University Press, 2002)

MILLNER, JACQUELINE, 'André Chénier's Astonishing Revolutionary Language in the "Iambs"', *Dalhousie French Studies*, 57 (Winter 2001), 10–24

MONTAIGNE, MICHEL DE, *Essais*, ed. by P. Villey and V. L. Saulnier, 3 vols (Paris: Presses universitaires de France, 1965)

OERGEL, MAIKE, *Zeitgeist — How Ideas Travel: Politics, Culture and the Public in the Age of Revolution* (Berlin: De Gruyter, 2019)

PALMER, R. R., *Twelve Who Ruled: The Year of the Terror in the French Revolution* (Princeton, NJ: Princeton University Press, 1941)

PASCAL, JEAN-NOËL (ed.), *Lectures d'André Chénier: Imitations et préludes poétiques, Art d'aimer, Élégies* (Rennes: Presses universitaires de Rennes, 2005)

PAULIN, TOM, *The Road to Inver: Translations, Versions, Imitations 1975–2003* (London: Faber & Faber, 2004)

PEARSON, ROGER, *Unacknowledged Legislators: The Poet as Lawgiver in Post-revolutionary France* (Oxford: Oxford University Press, 2016)

PETTERSON, JAMES, *Poetry Proscribed: Twentieth-century (Re)Visions of the Trials of Poetry in France* (Lewisburg, PA: Bucknell University Press, 2008)

PHYTHIAN, B. A. (ed.), *Considering Poetry: An Approach to Criticism* (London: Hodder & Stoughton, 2004)

QUILLEN, ELISABETH, 'L'Idée de liberté dans la pensée et la poésie d'André Chénier', *Neohelicon*, 1.3–4 (September 1973), 351–63

RITZ, OLIVIER, *Les Métaphores naturelles dans le débat sur la Révolution* (Paris: Classiques Garnier, 2017)

ROSÁRIO PONTES, MARIA DO, 'André Chénier et la poésie cosmogonique', *Repositório Aberto da Universidade do Porto* (1993), 163–77 <http://hdl.handle.net/10216/7968> [accessed 21 November 2020]

ROUSSEAU, JEAN-JACQUES, 'Essai sur l'origine des langues', in *Œuvres complètes de Jean-Jacques Rousseau*, 13 vols (Paris: Hachette, 1905), I, 370–408

SCARFE, FRANCIS, *André Chénier: His Life and Work, 1762–1794* (Oxford: Clarendon Press, 1965)

SCOTT, CLIVE, *French Verse-art: A Study* (Cambridge: Cambridge University Press, 1980)

—— *The Work of Literary Translation* (Cambridge: Cambridge University Press, 2018)

SETH, CATRIONA, *André Chénier: le miracle du siècle* (Paris: Presses de l'Université Paris-Sorbonne, 2005)

——'"Inscrire sa mémoire aux fastes d'Hélicon": poéthique d'André Chénier', *Revue d'histoire littéraire de la France*, 119.4 (2019), 801–20

SHELLEY, PERCY BYSSHE, *A Defence of Poetry*, in *Shelley's Poetry and Prose*, ed. by Donald H. Reiman and Neil Fraistat, 2nd edn (New York & London: Norton, 2002)

SMERNOFF, RICHARD, *André Chénier* (Boston: Twayne, 1977)

WAHNICH, SOPHIE, *La Liberté ou la mort: essai sur la Terreur et le terrorisme* (Paris: La Fabrique, 2003)

WALTER, GÉRARD, *André Chénier: son milieu et son temps* (Paris: Robert Laffont, 1947)

WORDSWORTH, WILLIAM, *Lyrical Ballads, with Pastoral and Other Poems*, 2nd edn, 2 vols (London: T. N. Longman and O. Rees, 1802)

INDEX

❖